P9-CNF-720

Roland Penrose

Portrait of Picasso

Published by The Museum of Modern Art, New York

Distributed by Simon and Schuster, New York

Picasso: *Self-portrait*. 1904
(Indian ink and water-colour, $6\frac{1}{2} \times 4$).
Col. Dora Maar.
Reproduced from
Pablo Picasso, Aquarelle und Gouachen
by John Richardson,
published by Holbein-Verlag AG.
Ektachrome by André Thevenet, Paris

Trustees of the Museum of Modern Art

John Hay Whitney, *Chairman of the Board*; Henry Allen Moe,
1*st Vice-Chairman*; Nelson A. Rockefeller, *2nd Vice-Chairman*;
William A. M. Burden, *President*; Mrs David M. Levy,
1*st Vice-President*; Alfred H. Barr, Jr., Mrs Roberts Woods Bliss,
Stephen C. Clark, Ralph F. Colin, Mrs W. Murray Crane,*
René d'Harnoncourt, Mrs Edsel B. Ford, Philip L. Goodwin,
A. Conger Goodyear, Mrs Simon Guggenheim,*
Wallace K. Harrison, Mrs Walter Hochschild,
James W. Husted,* Mrs Albert D. Lasker, Mrs Henry R. Luce,
Ranald H. Macdonald, Mrs Samuel A. Marx,
Mrs G. Macculloch Miller, William S. Paley,
Mrs Bliss Parkinson, Mrs Charles S. Payson, Duncan Phillips,*
Andrew Carnduff Ritchie, David Rockefeller,
Mrs John D. Rockefeller, 3rd, Beardsley Ruml,* Paul J. Sachs,*
John L. Senior, Jr., James Thrall Soby,
Edward M. M. Warburg, Monroe Wheeler.

*Honorary Trustee for Life

Printed in England by Percy Lund, Humphries & Co. Ltd
Bradford and London

Published in the United States of America in 1957
by the Museum of Modern Art, New York

All rights reserved

Library of Congress Catalogue Card Number 57-7372

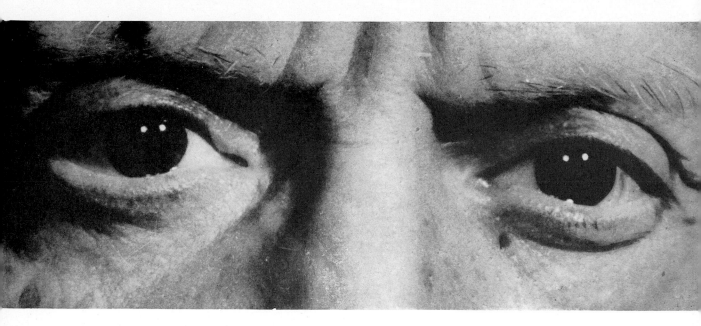

Contents

Preface by Alfred H. Barr, Jr.

Suppose the camera had been invented 500 years before Picasso. Think what photographs we might have had! Ghiberti standing beside his prize-winning relief for the Baptistry doors ('third from the left, with the disgruntled expression, is Brunelleschi, the runner-up'); Grand Duke Basil Dmitrevich handing Andrei Rublyov the contract for the new frescoes in the Cathedral of the Dormition; 'Petrus Christus Paints a Picture' – a series of documentary photographs with captions by Antonello da Messina; Michelangelo, perched on his scaffolding under the Sistine ceiling, his beard clotted with plaster, shouting his anger at Pope Julius down below; or, finally, and just to settle a long argument, Hubert van Eyck, himself, at work on the Ghent altarpiece.

How Picasso will ultimately rank with these heroes of the past we cannot be sure. There may even be a few stubborn eccentrics who would deny that he is the greatest contemporary artist. But no one can convincingly refute the statement that he is far and away the most photographed of living artists. As evidence of this one may point to the number of photographs Roland Penrose has chosen for this volume, and even more to the hundreds he has had to omit.

Why is Picasso so continually subject to photography? Because he is an immensely famous artist? A controversial figure? Yes, of course. But there are other reasons which have little to do with his reputation, though much to do with his personality and appearance.

As many of our best photographers have discovered, Picasso is extraordinarily interesting to watch: when he is gay he is irresistibly charming; when he is angry his eyes seem diabolical; even when he is morose or bored his face is arresting.

And, apparently, Picasso likes to be photographed. Sometimes, it is true, he has turned on a persistent snapshooter with fury, but ordinarily he seems as obliging to photographers as a movie star or a political candidate. He will even put on a comical act with a false moustache, trick spectacles or a cowboy hat as if he felt that his ordinary appearance were not sufficient. Yet Picasso needs no publicity and his self-esteem is fed to surfeit in a dozen other ways. Watching him being photographed one feels that he is behaving much as he does when one sees him receiving time-wasting guests or looking over the drawings of some young artist. He seems moved primarily by a deep sense of courtesy rather than by vanity.

This book is, of course, not limited to images of Picasso. Pictures of his ancestors, his relatives, his many studios, his friends, the women he loved, his children, combine to document the background and foreground of his life. Assembled by the editor after long and diligent search, they are presented here with exceptional authority.

Roland Penrose is a painter, a poet, an essayist, an organizer of highly original exhibitions, and by far the most adventurous English collector of his generation. During the past thirty-five years he has lived much in France and has come to know Picasso intimately. Though recently he has done extensive research in preparation for his forthcoming biography of the artist, his approach is essentially that of a devoted friend. It is very fitting that *Portrait of Picasso,* which Roland Penrose and his publishers planned as a salute to Pablo Picasso on his seventy-fifth birthday, should be the work of a man whose scholarship is warmed and deepened by an affectionate personal understanding of his subject.

The material in this book has been collected in connection with an exhibition entitled Picasso Himself *organized by Roland Penrose and first held in 1956 at the Institute of Contemporary Arts of London on the occasion of the seventy-fifth birthday of Pablo Picasso and later, amended, in connection with the exhibition held from May to September 1957 at The Museum of Modern Art, New York.*

Foreword

It is now seventy-five years since Pablo Picasso was born in Malaga. He now lives at Cannes and the fame of his creative work is known throughout the world. It has been my purpose in this study to give a visual record of the life of Picasso by assembling portraits, sketches, photographs, and documents which have a direct bearing on the artist himself, his friends, and his surroundings up to the present time. It is my belief that, although it cannot be complete, this may serve as a background against which it will become easier to understand both the revolutionary changes that have taken place periodically and the less obvious stream of continuity that runs persistently through his work.

This biographical survey has been made possible in the first place by the co-operation of the artist himself, to whom I am greatly indebted for material hitherto unpublished and much essential information. Many of his friends have also generously contributed valuable documents and advice. In particular Monsieur Jaime Sabartès has been throughout an unfailing source of information. My thanks are also due to Mr Alfred H. Barr, author of one of the most comprehensive works on Picasso,* M. Jean Cocteau, M. Daniel-Henry Kahnweiler, M. André Lefevre, M. Tristan Tzara, and M. Christian Zervos who have known him intimately for many years, M. Paul Picasso, the artist's elder son, also M. Heinz Berggruen, M. and Mme Georges Bernier, M. Gérald Cramer, Louis Dalmas, Mme Paul Eluard, Mr Eric Estorick, Dr Bernhard Geiser, Mlle Françoise Gilot, Sidney Janis, Mme Renée Laporte, Comdr and Mrs E. Heywood-Lonsdale, Mme Yvonne Lyon, Mlle Dora Maar, Mr Man Ray, M. H. Matarasso, Mr Jacques O'Hana, Mr John Richardson, M. Siegfried Rosengart, Mrs Howard Samuel, and Mr James Thrall Soby, who have given invaluable help and in many cases generously allowed access to material from their collections.

It is thanks to the collaboration of a number of distinguished photographers that a composite portrait of Picasso can be made. In this connection I wish to express my gratitude to Cecil Beaton, Hjalmar Boyesen, Brian Brake, Robert Capa, Henri Cartier Bresson, John Deakin, Robert Doisneau, Douglas Glass, Alexander Liberman, Dora Maar, Man Ray, Gjon Mili, Lee Miller, Inge Morath, Peter Rose Pulham, Jacqueline Roque, Sanford H. Roth, André Thevenet, and André Villers.

* ALFRED H. BARR, Jr. *Picasso. Fifty Years of his Art.* 1946. The Museum of Modern Art, New York.

8

Introduction

In 1881, Pablo Picasso was born at Malaga into a world very different from that in which we live today; but we have grown accustomed to spectacular and dramatic changes with unexpected ease, and discoveries which at that date seemed incredible are now considered commonplace. Man has been borne along at a dizzy speed into the hazards and wonders of the atomic age. The advances of science have been welcomed greedily with little thought as to their consequences and new and more dazzling inventions are awaited with the eagerness of a child hoping for a new toy. It is, however, noticeable that society has not greeted with equal enthusiasm the revolution that has happened during the same period in the arts. Here, every development has been received with violent and stubborn opposition. The work of all advanced artists has been associated with blasphemy, indecency, insanity, and immorality. Politically it has been considered to be a symbol of treason: witness the cries of *sales Boches* at the first performance of *Parade* in Paris in 1917, and the term 'Bolshevik Art' which paradoxically has been used to describe those forms of art that have been severely discouraged in the U.S.S.R. for more than thirty years.

Accepting and even enjoying the innovations of science, the artist has still continued to perform his ancient function, the discovery of new forms of expression. The refusal of society to admit the validity of his work has in no way deterred him. It has on the contrary added zest.

In the last decade however, the situation has changed. Already it is difficult to remember how violent was the struggle. The work of those who rebelled is now shown in places of honour and the term *avant garde* is ceasing to retain its former meaning. The talent and imagination of the pioneers is still evident but it is easy to forget their courage and the challenge they made to basic problems of aesthetics and the relationship between art and life. The accepted conceptions of good taste, common sense, and beauty which in 1881 were revered as yardsticks by which society could safely form its judgements have been questioned. Even beauty itself is now uncertain of its name. But the wearied and discredited concepts of the past have not been destroyed by theorists and scholars but by the creative work of artists who have discovered new means of expression and opened our eyes to new forms of vision.

A movement of such consequence can only happen when a direction is given to it by men of genius. The past seventy-five years have

1. Birthplace of Pablo Picasso,
Plaza de la Merced, Malaga.
Photo by Lee Miller

2. Pablo, aged 4. (Translation of note
by Picasso: 'Vermilion red costume,
gold buttons, bronze shoes'.)

3. Pablo, aged 7, and his sister Lola.
(Translation of note by Picasso:
'Lola's dress; black with blue belt,
white collar. Myself; white costume,
navy blue overcoat, blue beret'.)

4. Art School of San Telmo, Malaga.
Photos by Lee Miller.

5. Painting by Don José Ruiz Blasco.

in fact been made exceptionally rich by the work of painters who have contributed in various ways to the history of contemporary art, but no single man has influenced this revolution more profoundly than PABLO PICASSO.

So important to us at the present time are the many aspects of the work of this prodigious artist that, rather than wait for the balanced judgement of posterity and at the risk of failing to place each detail in its proper perspective, we have taken here the unusual course of making a visual survey of the life and work up to the present time of an artist who is still alive, and refuse to admit, even though there are bound to be omissions, that it is in any way premature.

Picasso, in voluntary exile in France, has become more widely known during his lifetime than any painter throughout history. This achievement is all the more notable when we rember the scorn with which his early discoveries were greeted. It is a phenomenon that must be of interest to all students of human life.

6. Picasso: *The Matador*. Earliest known painting by Picasso. 1889–90 (oil).

Photographers, Biographers

Picasso is above all preoccupied with vision and it is therefore appropriate that a visual record should be made of the surroundings in which he was born and in which he has chosen to live, the friends he has made and the women who have shared his intimacy. By so doing we can gain insight into both his work and his character, we can divine the influences that have combined to inspire him and perhaps shed some light on the strange and incalculable workings of genius.

7. Picasso: *Portrait of Don José, the artist's father*. 1895 (water-colour).

A visual record of the life of Picasso became increasingly easy to establish as time passed owing to the development of photography. Although in early days photographs are scarce and many events passed unrecorded, the ubiquitous camera now provides a surplus of images from which to select. It is fortunate that Picasso himself is usually not unwilling to be photographed and even more important that several distinguished photographers have become his close friends.

8

9

12

10

13

14

11

15

Pablo Picasso

born Malaga 1881

14

16. Picasso: *Portrait of Don José*. 1895. (Water-colour with inscription, 'To my dear Antonio Muñoz Degrain, I send this Christmas present with my affection. P. Ruiz Picasso 12.95' – Translation.) Muñoz Degrain was a painter well known throughout Spain, a resident of Malaga, and a friend of the family. Municipal Museum, Malaga.

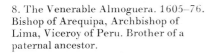

8. The Venerable Almoguera. 1605–76. Bishop of Arequipa, Archbishop of Lima, Viceroy of Peru. Brother of a paternal ancestor.

9. Brother Pedro de Cristo Almoguera. 1773–1855. Lived as a hermit in the mountains of Cordova. Brother of a paternal ancestor. The flowers were painted on the frame by Picasso's father.

10. Don Diego Ruiz de Almoguera, *grandfather* of Picasso. Born in Cordova, 1799; lived in Malaga.

11. Don José Ruiz Blasco, *father of* Picasso. Born in Malaga c.1850, died in Barcelona in 1913. Painter and art master in Malaga, Coruña, and Barcelona.

12. Doña Maria Guardeno. *Great-grandmother* of Picasso.

13. Don Francisco Picasso Guardeno. Born in Malaga and went to school in England. Became a customs officer in Havana where he died in 1883. *Grandfather* of Picasso.

14. Doña Inez Lopez Robles. *Grandmother* of Picasso. Lived in Malaga.

15. Doña Maria Picasso de Ruiz. Born in Malaga in 1855, died in Barcelona in 1939. *Mother* of Picasso.

17. Picasso: *Portrait of the artist's mother*; drawn soon after their arrival in Barcelona in 1895 (pastel).

18. Picasso, aged 15. Barcelona, 1896.

Origins and early youth

The story of the origins, infancy, and youth of this child with piercing black eyes, born with an irrepressible desire to draw and paint, is told by Picasso's old friend, Jaime Sabartès.* He has unearthed from documents the existence among Pablo's ancestors of austere dignitaries of the church, and revealed remote descent on the paternal side from the fifteenth-century hidalgos of the Spanish

19. Picasso: *Portrait of Lola*. 1898
(pastel $16 \times 11\frac{1}{4}$).
Col. Mrs Howard Samuel.

province of Léon. On the side of Pablo's mother, whose family name
was Picasso, Sabartès has recently discovered links with a fashionable Genoese portrait painter of the early eighteenth century,
Matteo Picasso. But there is still some doubt as to the Italian origins
of Picasso, and as far as both branches of the family can be followed
with any certainty they were predominantly Andalusian.

* JAIME SABARTÈS. *Picasso, Documents Iconographiques*. Pierre Cailler (Geneva,
1954).

17

20. Ruiz: *Portrait of Pablo Ruiz Picasso* by a friend in Barcelona, 1896 (oil).

21. Picasso: *Self-portrait in eighteenth-century costume*. Barcelona, 1896 (oil).

The family left Malaga, the birthplace of Pablo, when he was 10. Three years later at Coruna his father, Don José Ruiz Blasco, an honourable bourgeois painter in the academic tradition and art master in the local institute, finding that he was outstripped by his son in his own art, handed over to him once and for ever his paints and brushes. The speed with which Pablo's talent developed and the ease with which he subsequently astonished his examiners in the more exacting academies of the fine arts in Barcelona and Madrid suggest that he would have had no trouble in finding for himself an easy road to success. But disregarding the advice of his family, the infant prodigy chose to become *l'enfant terrible*.

Barcelona and 'Els quatre gats'

After four years in Coruna, Don José obtained a post as professor in the School of Fine Arts in Barcelona. The family, consisting of Pablo's parents, his sister Lola, who often sat for her brother as a model, and himself, moved to this city, which being near the

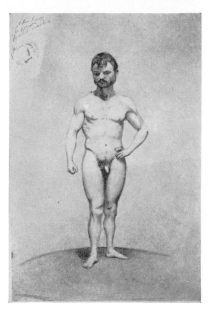

22. Picasso: *Portrait of Don José*. 1896.

23. Picasso: *Diploma drawing for the entrance examination to the School of Fine Arts* (*La Lonja*). Barcelona, 1895 (lead pencil).

24. Picasso: *Self-portrait*. Barcelona, 1896 (lead pencil).

25. Picasso: *Science and Charity*. 1896 (oil). Picasso's father set this subject and posed for the seated doctor. From the collection of the artist's sister, Barcelona.

26. Diploma of 'Honourable Mention' awarded at the Exhibition of Fine Arts, Madrid, 1897, for the painting *Science and Charity*.

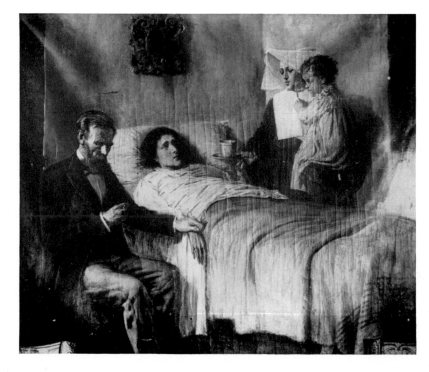

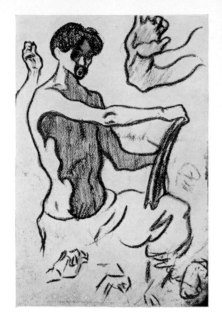

28. Horta de San Juan. After falling ill in Madrid, Picasso spent several months in the spring of 1898 at the house of his friend Manuel Pallares.

29. Cave in the mountains near Horta. Picasso lived here for a while with Pallares.

27. Picasso: *Self-portrait*. Barcelona, 1897 (charcoal).

30. Picasso: *Caricature of Rusiñol and Casas*. 1901 (pen and coloured crayon, $5\frac{1}{2} \times 3\frac{1}{2}$). O'Hana Gallery, London.

31. Interior of 'Els Quatre Gats'. c.1899.

32. Picasso: *Poster for 'Els Quatre Gats'*. 1898. Portraits of (left to right) Pere Romeu, Picasso, Rocarol, Fontbona, Angel F. de Soto, Sabartès (pen and ink).

20

33. Picasso: *Poeta Decadente*. Portrait of Jaime Sabartès. 1899 (charcoal and pastel, 18½ × 12¼). Col. Jaime Sabartès.

34. Opisso: *Picasso and Pere Romeu at Sitges*. 1898.

French frontier was more closely in touch with intellectual move-ments abroad. Pablo had no difficulty in passing the entrance tests for an academic career, but found very soon that he had nothing more to learn from his teachers. The lonely path of self-discovery and the consequences of his own unusual powers led him towards a small group of poets and painters. These Catalan intellectuals had founded an ephemeral, revolutionary tavern, 'a Gothic beer hall for those amorous of the North', known as *Els Quatre Gats*, the Four Cats. In their bohemian company the prevailing attitude was a

21

35. Picasso: *Part of a letter to the poet Ramón Reventos*. Paris, 9 November 1900.

desperate anarchic desire to rebel against the existing order, combined with a *fin de siècle* decadence and an urge to suffer as *le poète maudit* in order to prove their complete integrity. The group was led by the artist-playwright Santiago Rusiñol, the critic Miguel Utrillo, the fashionable portraitist Ramon Casas, and the painter of outcasts Isidro Nonell. They accepted as their host the genial entertainer Pere Romeu and attracted around them the most talented and arrogant youth of the city. Among them, Picasso made the acquaintance of the painters Ramón Pichot, Ricardo Opisso, Sebastian Junyer-Vidal, Juan Vidal Ventosa, Ricardo Canals, the sculptor Manolo Hugué, and the poets Ramón Reventos and Jaime Sabartès. Although he continued to live with his family he showed a degree of independence in his work which led him away from the academic traditions of his father and towards the discovery of a new school of painting.

In spite of their native pride, the aspirations of the Catalonian intellectuals turned towards the achievements of artists and poets in France, England, Scandinavia, and Germany. Following this current, Picasso paid his first visit to Paris in the autumn of 1900. His companion was a painter, Carlos Casagemas, whose career was

36. 49 rue Gabrielle, Paris. Picasso lived here during his first visit to Paris, 1900. It was formerly the studio of the Catalan painter Nonell.

37. Picasso: *Self-portrait with Casagemas*. 1899.

38. Picasso: *Self-portrait*. 1901. Soon after the second arrival in Paris. The figure with a beard smoking a pipe is Jaume Andreu Bonsons. In the background is the Moulin Rouge with the price of entry announced as three francs. The writing up the side of the drawing is not by Picasso (pen and coloured crayon, 7 × 4½). Col. Mrs E. Heywood-Lonsdale.

39. Casas: *Portrait of Picasso*. Reproduced in *Pel y Ploma*, Barcelona,
June 1901, to illustrate the first review of an exhibition of Picasso's pastels
by Miguel Utrillo. In the background on the right is one of the windmills
of Montmartre and on the left a theatre in Barcelona.

40. Picasso: *Self-portrait with Jaume Andreu Bonsons, who travelled with Picasso on his second visit to Paris.* 1901 (pen and coloured crayon).

41. Picasso: *The Blue Room.* 1901 (oil, $20 \times 24\frac{1}{2}$). Phillips Collection, Washington. Picasso's studio at 130ter Boulevard de Clichy. On the wall hangs Toulouse Lautrec's poster of May Milton.

42. Picasso (seated) in his studio, Boulevard de Clichy, 1901. On his right is his friend Petrus Manach, and on his left Fuentes Torres and his wife. The inscription says: 'Me in the studio. Au revoir.'

43. Picasso: *Self-portrait in top hat.* Paris, 1901.

brought abruptly to an end by suicide due to unrequited love. Picasso was left to find his own friends among the Spanish and French artists who frequented Montmartre.

For the next four years, he divided his time between Barcelona, Madrid, and Paris. At an earlier date he had visited the Spanish capital to study at the Royal Academy of San Fernando, but after a brilliant entrance, disillusionment and illness soon caused him to return to Barcelona. His second visit in the spring of 1901 was in the company of a Catalan writer, Francisco de Assis Soler, with whom he made a brief attempt to launch *Arte Joven*, a journal of which

44. Picasso: *Self-portrait with Francisco de Assis Soler*. 1901. Drawing from *Arte Joven* announcing *Madrid*, a review which never appeared. Picasso was to have been art editor and Soler the editor. (Crayon.)

45. Picasso: *Group of artists in Madrid*. 1901. Left to right: unknown, Cornuti, Francisco de Assis Soler, Picasso, Alberto Lozano (crayon).

46. Picasso: *Self-portrait*. Paris, 1901 (oil, $31\frac{7}{8} \times 23\frac{5}{8}$). Owned by the artist.

Picasso made himself the art editor and sole illustrator of the two rare numbers that appeared. Again, Madrid failed to provide the stimulus he required, and he left within a few months for Paris, his real spiritual home. The prestige and the turbulent atmosphere of this centre of the arts induced him to move permanently to the French capital in 1904. By then, a temperament of restless inquiry had helped him to discover and absorb the great variety of styles, ancient and contemporary, that he found on view in the museums and dealers' galleries. With the originality of one who can understand and interpret the work of others and yet preserve in his own

47. Picasso: *Self-portrait with Angel F. de Soto and Sebastian Junyer-Vidal.* 1902 (pen and ink).

48. Picasso: *Self-portrait on beach.* 1902 (pen and coloured crayon).

49. Picasso: *Self-portrait with nude and S. Junyer-Vidal.* 1901. A parody of Manet's *Olympia.*

50. Picasso: *Self portrait.* 1902 (brush and ink). The writing at the top of the drawing is not by Picasso.

51. Picasso: *Letter to Max Jacob from Barcelona*. 1902 (pen and ink, $10\frac{1}{2} \times 8\frac{1}{4}$). Below: The figure in front of the bull ring is a self-portrait. Above: On the reverse of the same letter is a drawing of the horses that drag away the dead bull after the fight. Collection Gérald Cramer, Geneva.

52. Picasso: *Halleluiah*. 1904. A description in drawings of a journey to Paris in April 1904 with S. Junyer-Vidal for whom he prophesies success.

Translation of titles. (1) *They reach the frontier in a third-class carriage.* (2) *At one o'clock they have arrived and say: 'Cony, qué salado!'* (3) *They arrive at Montauban wrapped in their overcoats.* (4) *And at nine, they arrive at Paris at last.* (6) *He gets to Duran-Rouel [sic] and he gives him a lot of cash.*

53. Picasso in Paris, 1904, with the inscription, *A mes chers amis Suzanne et Henri (Bloch)*.

54. Windows of Picasso's studio, 'Le Bateau Lavoir'. The arrows were drawn by Picasso. Translation of note 'Windows of my studio 13 rue Ravignon'.

55. Picasso: *Drawing, heading a letter from Max Jacob to Mme Suzanne Bloch, wife of the musician Henri Bloch.* 1905. Left to right: portraits of Mme Bloch, Max Jacob, Picasso, and their cat.

56. Max Jacob in front of his lodgings in Montmartre. Wearing the top hat that he shared with Picasso.

work the strength of its individuality, he passed through the many influences around him, developing his own style with unceasing vigour. During the period of transition between Spain and France, the early subject matter emanating from the atmosphere of the Moulin Rouge gave way to the ghostlike outcasts from the streets and cafés of Barcelona and Paris. Their forms were bathed in a blueness which gave rise to these paintings being classified as the Blue Period. Instinctively, Picasso disliked exhibiting his work at the yearly salons, even in company with the more revolutionary groups, but at first in Barcelona and later in Paris dealers offered to show his work. They were rewarded by the immediate enthusiasm of a few enlightened critics. Max Jacob, who at the time was writing art criticism, was so struck on the opening day of Picasso's first exhibition in Paris at the gallery of Ambroise Vollard that he went at once to Picasso's studio to make his acquaintance. Their understanding of each other in spite of language difficulties was immediate. The character of the poet, both waggish and passionate, was congenial to the eager curiosity of his friend. Their meeting was the beginning of a lifelong intimacy, and the first link in the chain of friendships which extended to Guillaume Apollinaire, André Salmon, Alfred Jarry, Pierre Reverdy, Maurice Raynal and many other poets. Instinctively they found their way to Picasso's studio in Montmartre. This comfortless abode formed part of a strange dilapidated building known in derision as the *Bateau Lavoir*, but according to Salmon it should have had inscribed above the door, *Au rendez-vous des poètes*. Picasso joined this hive of struggling artists in 1904. He lived, worked, and entertained his friends there until he moved in 1909 to larger and less bohemian quarters in the nearby Boulevard de Clichy.

Although in his friendships Picasso has more often sought the company of poets than of painters, from early days, the 'Bande Picasso' included, among his compatriots, the sculptors Manolo (Hugué), Gargallo, Gonzales, and the painters Pichot and Canals. In the early days of Cubism it was joined by Juan Gris. Matisse, Derain, Léger, the Douanier Rousseau, and Marie Laurencin, the mistress of Apollinaire, were all familiar visitors, but the friendship among painters that proved to be of the greatest importance has also been the longest to survive. The name of Georges Braque must always be associated with that of Picasso in the great discoveries that led the Cubist movement to its height in the years between 1908 and 1914.

The life in this circle of talented youth was of a rare intensity.

57. Fernande Olivier and Picasso in Montmartre. *c*.1906.

58. Picasso, Fernande Olivier, and the writer Ramon Reventos in Barcelona. 1906. Photo by Vidal Ventosa.

59. Fernande Olivier. *c*.1906.

60. André Salmon: *Portrait of Picasso*. 1908 (ink and water-colour, 8 × 5½). Col. Picasso.

61. Picasso: *André Salmon*. 1907 (pen and ink).

62. Picasso: *Portrait of Fernande Olivier*. *c*.1906.

63. Fernande Olivier: *Portrait of Picasso. c.* 1908.

64. Derain: *Portrait of Picasso.* 1908 (ink, $8\frac{1}{4} \times 6\frac{1}{2}$) with the inscription '*mon portrait fait par André Derain*'. Col. Picasso.

65. Picasso dressed in the uniform of Georges Braque. 1909.

67. Picasso: *Gertrude Stein.* 1906 (oil, 39×32). Metropolitan Museum of Art, New York.

66. Gertrude Stein. *c.*1906. Gertrude Stein Collection, Yale University.

Enthusiasm, energy, boisterous enjoyment, and brilliant but relentless humour were balanced by an overwhelming dedication to work based upon jealous and passionate love. Raynal, Salmon, Gertrude Stein, and Fernande Olivier describe a strange variety of events, such as the banquet given in honour of the Douanier Rousseau in Picasso's studio, the expeditions to the Lapin Agile, to the Cirque Medrano, or across the Seine to the literary hierarchy of the Closerie des Lilas. These were punctuated by the weekly dinner parties given by the Steins which were attended by a well-picked cosmopolitan array of talent. Owing to the rarity of photographs in the years preceding the twenties, however, there are no visual records of these events, nor even of the interior of the 'Bateau Lavoir', with its stacks of freshly painted canvases. Even later, in 1917, there are no photos of Picasso's wedding, at which Apollinaire and Max Jacob were witnesses. But this scarcity is balanced, in addition to his

68. Marie Laurençin: *Portrait of Picasso.*
*c.*1908 (oil, $16\frac{1}{4} \times 13$).
Col. Mme Yvonne Lyon.

69. Picasso: *Letter to Leo Stein thanking him for an invitation to lunch, with drawing 'Une très belle danse barbare'.* 1905.

70. Picasso: *Self-portrait with Egyptian crown.* 1901. O'Hana Gallery, London. The Douanier Rousseau is said to have told Picasso: 'We are the greatest painters of our time, you in the Egyptian style, I in the modern.'

71. Picasso: *Harlequin.*
1905 (oil, $39\frac{3}{8} \times 39$).

35

production of great numbers of finished drawings and portraits, by Picasso's habit of making rapid sketches and caricatures of himself and his friends. These vivid images continue as a record until Picasso temporarily abandoned realistic drawing during the Cubist period. It is through them, as well as through the drawings that his friends made of him, that we can still see clearly the features of Picasso and the intensity of his expression, centred in the unchanging blackness of his eyes. Through these lively records we can understand better his passion for Fernande Olivier, who shared with

72. Picasso: *Self portrait*. 1903 (pen and ink, $10\frac{1}{2} \times 7\frac{3}{4}$). Private collection, London. This is a sketch for the painting *La Vie*, 1903, now in the Cleveland Museum of Art.

him the years of poverty, his friendship for Gertrude Stein, and his enjoyment of the fertile companionship of Apollinaire and Max Jacob.

We can trace also the close association between the artist and the characters of his own invention. Just as under the instruction of his father he painted Don José as the doctor in the early set piece *Science and Charity* (see plate 25), so he sees himself later among the blind beggars and the absinthe drinkers. His most persistent impersonation at that time was Harlequin (see plate 71). Later, after the change of mood which coincides with his settling in Paris and his love for Fernande Olivier, that change which led him to turn from the pathos of the Blue Period to the more serene detachment of the circus folk and the 'Saltimbanques', Harlequin reappears intermittently as a self-portrait, until finally all direct likeness vanishes and only the diamond shapes of his costume continue to reveal his presence in Cubism.

73. Picasso: *Self-portrait*. 1906 (oil, 36 × 28). Philadelphia Museum of Art.

74. Picasso: *Self-portrait*. 1907 (oil).

Les Demoiselles d'Avignon

In the spring of 1907, Picasso showed his friends the large and astonishing canvas freshly and rapidly painted with his usual impetuosity which has since become known as *Les Demoiselles d'Avignon*. The shock to all who saw it was unforgettable. At first no one understood what he was doing. He overheard Matisse and Leo Stein laughing behind his back. Braque is reported to have

75. Picasso: *Portrait of Max Jacob.* 1907 (gouache).

remarked that it was as if Picasso wished them to exchange their normal diet for one of tow and paraffin. His most devoted friends could only gape and advise him not to continue in this vein. Poets, painters, patrons, and dealers, with not more than one or two exceptions, disapproved profoundly. They regretted sadly such 'a loss to French art'.

In his solitude Picasso stood unshaken and as time went on he had the satisfaction of seeing his friends begin to realize that this picture was a landmark in the history of contemporary art. He had had the courage to risk everything and question the meaning of beauty itself. That he should be thought mad, left him indifferent, but that he should be considered dangerous, he knew was just. His change of style was profound and consistent. It is reflected in two self-portraits, one painted in 1906 and the other a year later (see plates 73 and 74).

The birth of a new style

The Blue period came to an end in 1904, and with an increasing consciousness of the importance of primitive art and of Cézanne, the energy and imagination of Picasso led him through successive stages of development, now classified as the Rose and Negro periods. It seemed incredible that he could enjoy the company of so many friends, work so long at night, sleep so late, produce such a vast quantity of work, and retain unbounded curiosity in all that went on around him.

By the autumn of 1909, Picasso had become known, both in Paris and abroad, as a young painter of exceptional talent. His earnings allowed him to move to a more spacious and comfortable studio where he had room to hang on the walls his acquisitions and gifts from his friends. Among them were Matisse's portrait of his daughter Marguerite and finds that he had made which included African masks, paintings by the Douanier Rousseau, a small Corot, with strange objects that fascinated him regardless of their value. With his friends he continued to frequent by night the gas lit entertainments of Montmartre.

During the summer, Picasso followed the custom usual among artists of leaving Paris and choosing a quiet place in the country to work. On his return in the autumn of 1908 from a visit to La Rue des Bois, north of Paris, with a large quantity of landscape, still life, and figure paintings, he found that Braque had brought back from L'Estaque a series of landscapes in a similar style that earned at the Salon d'Automne, the derisive title, 'Cubist'. From then on

76. Interior of 11 Boulevard de Clichy with the painter Pichot, 1910 or 1911. At the top of the photograph part of Matisse's portrait of his daughter can be seen; below it is the first negro mask bought by Picasso, to the left is a landscape of Horta by Pallarès, and a cubist drawing by Picasso.

77. Picasso with cat, 1910 or 1911. Behind him there is a reproduction of Ingres' *Odalisque* and a fragment of Aubusson tapestry, and beside him a guitar.

78. 11 Boulevard de Clichy. Picasso's studio from 1909–12.

79. Fernande Olivier with the niece of Manuel Pallarès Grau at Horta de San Juan. 1909.

80. Interior of Picasso's studio at Horta de San Juan. 1909.

81. Maison Delcros, Céret. Picasso stayed at this house in Céret in the summers of 1911, 1912, 1913. Photo by Robert Julia.

Picasso and Braque, in spite of the difference in their temperaments, became closely associated in their work, and others, particularly Fernand Léger and Juan Gris, began to explore the possibilities of this new form of art. Without desiring it, Picasso found himself acclaimed as the founder of a new school of painting, Cubism.

Several times he returned to Spain. Of these visits, one of the most productive was the summer he spent at Horta de San Juan with Fernande. The following year he went with Derain and Pichot to Cadaqués and in 1911 his old friend Manolo persuaded him to visit Céret. A group of friends, including Braque, Max Jacob, Juan Gris, Kisling, and others were already attracted by the charm of its mountain landscape. In 1912 and 1914, two memorable summers were spent in Provence, the first at Sorgues and the second at Avignon. In both cases Braque was living nearby.

Photographs taken during these years are still scarce, and portraits are completely lacking except for the imposing paintings by Picasso of a few chosen friends in the analytical Cubist style. As a result, there are no drawings of Eva (Marcelle Humbert), who became Picasso's companion when he separated from Fernande early in 1912. Her name or her synonym, *Ma Jolie*, however, appears inscribed in many Cubist paintings. Only two photographs of Eva are known. In one she is dressed in a kimono, bought for her by Picasso in Marseille, and in the other their dog, one of a long succession of dogs that have belonged to Picasso, sits at her feet.

82. Eva (Marcelle Humbert) with dog at Sorgues. 1912.

83. Cubist paintings in front of La Villa les Clochettes, Sorgues. 1912.

84. Georges Braque in his studio in Montmartre. 1910.

85. Photograph of D-H. Kahnweiler taken by Picasso in his studio at 11 Boulevard de Clichy. 1912.

86. Picasso: *Portrait of Daniel-Henry Kahnweiler*. 1910, autumn (oil, $39\frac{1}{4} \times 28\frac{1}{4}$). Col. Mrs Gilbert Chapman

Cubist portraits

Although at first sight the Cubist portraits are not easily recognizable as likenesses, Picasso required his models to sit for them at length and with the exception of the lighthearted *Portrait of Braque*, the portraits of Uhde, Vollard, and Kahnweiler are haunted by a resemblance to their sitters. There is also a pre-Cubist portrait of Clovis Sagot, a remarkable likeness in a style showing the influence of Cézanne. Its idiom is not difficult for us to understand. It was, however, thought to be unintelligible and was held up to ridicule when it was shown in London in the first Post Impressionist exhibition in

87. Juan Gris: *Portrait of Picasso*. 1912.

88. Gargallo: *Picasso*. Portrait bust made for a keystone over a doorway of the Del Bosque Theatre in Barcelona. 1917.

89. Picasso: *Portrait of Apollinaire*. 1913. Frontispiece to *Alcools*, poems published in Paris in 1913 (Mercure de France).

90. Modigliani: *Picasso*. 1915 (drawing, $10\frac{1}{4} \times 8\frac{3}{4}$). Col. Mme Renée Laporte.

the winter of 1910–11. Sagot, Uhde, Vollard, and Kahnweiler were all close friends of Picasso. They had in common among them that all had championed his painting, as connoisseurs and dealers, when others had completely failed to appreciate his work and treated him as a charlatan.

Outbreak of war in 1914

The departure of Braque from Avignon to join his regiment in August 1914 and Picasso's return later in the autumn to find that few of his friends were left in Paris, brought to an end the close association of the inventors of Cubism. Picasso has said that he never really found these friends again. He had already left Montmartre for a studio in the rue Schoelcher overlooking the Montparnasse cemetery when his sadness was increased by the death of Eva in the autumn of 1915.

91. Max Jacob: *Portrait of Picasso.* *c.*1917 (oil).

Max Jacob, physically unfit for military service, was still in Paris, but the absence of Apollinaire was a serious misfortune. Although Max Jacob had never been able to follow Picasso in his Cubist discoveries, and they slowly drifted apart, this did not prevent Picasso from becoming his godfather when Max Jacob became a Catholic in February 1915.

A few literary friends remained in Paris. Gertrude Stein recalls watching with Picasso the first zig-zag camouflage on guns passing along the Boulevard Raspail and quotes his remark 'We invented that'. Serge Férat and Roche Grey (Baroness Hélène d'Oettingen) who promoted the review *Les Soirées de Paris*, and later *Sic*,

92. Picasso with Max Jacob in front of the Café de la Rotonde, Boulevard du Montparnasse. 1915.

93. Picasso: *Max Jacob.* 1915 (lead pencil, $13 \times 9\frac{3}{4}$). Col. Dora Maar.

94. *The Imitation of Jesus Christ*, given to Max Jacob on the day of his baptism by Picasso who became his godfather. 1915.

41

95. G. de Chirico: *Picasso at table with*
(left to right) *the painter Léopold Survage,
Baroness d'Oettingen* (Roche Grey), *and
Serge Férat.* 1915. Above them hangs a
self-portrait by the Douanier Rousseau
(pen and ink, $12\frac{3}{4} \times 9\frac{1}{4}$).
Col. Eric Estorick.

96. Picasso: *The dining room at
Montrouge.* 1917 (lead pencil).

97–98. Picasso in his studio, 5 bis rue
Schoelcher. 1914 or 1915.

continued to entertain a few friends including, in the first year of
the war, the painters Giorgio de Chirico and Léopold Survage.

In 1916 Picasso moved to a small suburban house in Montrouge
where he continued to work, less oppressed by the wartime atmosphere of the capital.

The Russian Ballet

A diversion was brought about in the following year by the suggestion made by Jean Cocteau that Picasso should go with him to
Rome and make designs for the scenery and costumes for Cocteau's
new ballet *Parade* for which Eric Satie had written the music. This
introduction to the Russian Ballet of Serge Diaghileff brought with
it associations with a new circle of musicians, artists, and dancers.
Stravinsky, de Falla, Bakst, and Massine were working with
Diaghileff at the time, and among the troupe was a young dancer,
Olga Koklova, with whom Picasso fell in love and married a year
later.

The war took its toll. Both Braque and Apollinaire returned with
serious head wounds. In 1918, after a long convalescence, Apollinaire
died unexpectedly. Only a few months before, Picasso and Vollard
had been the witnesses at his wedding, and his loss was a heavy one
for Picasso to bear. They had met twelve years before and Apollinaire
had become the first critic to write in defence of Cubism. The genius
of Picasso had inspired him both as a poet and as a critic. In one of
his books, *Le Poète Assassiné*, he introduces his friend as a fantastic
sculptor to whom he gives the name 'l'Oiseau du Bénin' with
reference to Picasso's passion for African sculpture.

The move to the Rue la Boétie

Picasso's association with the Russian Ballet brought him into contact with the *élite* of an international circle of artists and patrons who
gave birth to the spectacular wave of creative activity following the
Armistice of 1918. He travelled with the Ballet to Barcelona in 1917
and to London for the production of *The Three Cornered Hat* with
his scenery and costumes in 1919. For several years he shared with
the rest of the world a sense of relaxation and enjoyed the beauty of
his young wife and his first born son, Paul (Paulo). He took a large
apartment in the Rue la Boétie. Next door Paul Rosenberg, who
became his dealer after the forced absence of Kahnweiler during the
war, opened his gallery. On the walls of the new apartment hung

99. Picasso: *Guillaume Apollinaire
wounded*. 1916 (lead pencil).
Col. André Lefevre.

100. Cocteau: *Portrait of Picasso as
'L'oiseau du Bénin' dedicated to
Apollinaire*. 1917 (lead pencil).

101. Picasso. 1917.

102. Picasso. 1916.

103. Picasso and Olga Koklova in Paris.
1917.

104. Picasso and Massine at Pompeii.
1917.

44

the paintings of Renoir, Cézanne, Rousseau, and Matisse that Picasso had acquired, and there Madame Picasso entertained their friends.

In 1919 Picasso went to stay with Madame Errazuriz in Biarritz and painted some murals for her in her villa. For nine years he had been deprived of the sea which he had enjoyed from childhood. During the following years, apart from one summer spent at Fontainebleau, he made long visits to places on the coast such as

105. Picasso: *Olga Koklova in Spanish costume.* 1917 (oil).

106. Picasso: *Self-portrait.* 1917.

107. Picasso. *Diaghileff and Selisbourg.* 1919 (crayon).

108. Picasso: *André Derain.* London, 1919. Derain designed the scenery for the ballet *La Boutique Fantasque*, first produced during the London season of 1919 (lead pencil).

109. Picasso: *Guillaume Apollinaire after he had received a head wound for which he was trepanned*. 1916. He died in November 1918 (pen and ink).

110. Picasso: *Jean Cocteau*. 1916 (lead pencil).

111. Picasso: *Ansermet, who conducted for the Russian ballet*. Barcelona, 1917 (lead pencil).

112. Picasso: *Leonide Massine*. London, 1919 (lead pencil).

113. Picasso: *Eric Satie*. 1920 (lead pencil).

114. Picasso: *Igor Stravinsky*. 1920 (lead pencil).

115. Picasso: *Léon Bakst*. 1922 (lead pencil).

117. Picasso: *Manuel de Falla*. 1920 (lead pencil)

116. Picasso with scene painters sitting on the drop curtain of *Parade*. Rome, 1917. This ballet was first produced by Serge Diaghileff in Paris in May 1917 and in London in 1919. The scenario was by Cocteau, music by Eric Satie, and costumes and scenery by Picasso.

118. Olga Picasso with Paulo. 1923.
Photo by Man Ray

119. 23 rue la Boétie, Paris. Picasso
moved to this two-floor apartment in
1919 and lived there till 1941.

120. Picasso: *Olga Picasso*. 1923 (oil).

121. Picasso with Paulo at Juan les Pins. 1925.

122. Paulo on a donkey. 1923.

123. Picasso. *Paulo on a donkey*. 1923 (coloured drawing).

124. Picasso. *Villa at Fontainebleau where Picasso spent the summer of* 1921 (lead pencil).

125. Picasso: *Interior of the villa at Fontainebleau*. 1921 (lead pencil)

126. Picasso: *The mother of the artist*. 1923 (oil).

127. Picasso in Barcelona surrounded by a group of friends. On his left is the painter Iturrino with whom Picasso shared his first exhibition at Vollard's gallery in 1901. At the back holding his hat is Muguel Utrillo. 1918.

128. Mme Picasso, Diaghileff, Edwin Evans, and Picasso at Monte Carlo. 1925.

129. Picasso: *Cocteau, Olga Picasso, Satie, and a friend at 23 rue la Boétie.* 1919 (lead pencil)

130. Picasso, Massine, and Diaghileff at Monte Carlo. 1925.

St Raphaël, Juan les Pins, Cap d'Antibes, Dinard, and Cannes. In 1924 he found Diaghileff and Massine with the music critic Edwin Evans at Monte Carlo and enjoyed the brilliant entertainment offered by Count Etienne de Beaumont both in Paris and on the Côte d'Azur. The discipline of Cubism yielded to scenes of arcadian delight and the splendour of stage designs for the ballet.

But Picasso had not forgotten his former discoveries nor did he fail to watch closely the rebellious 'Dada' movement led by Tristran Tzara and take interest in its successor, Surrealism. André Breton, Paul Eluard, Louis Aragon, Robert Desnos, Max Ernst, Joan Miró, and Man Ray were among the talented group of poets and painters who gave Surrealism its original impetus. But Picasso has never found it necessary in his art to limit himself to one style or one group of artists. His mastery of the medium allows him to use in the same day as many styles as he finds appropriate to his need for expression. In spite of frequent invitations, he remained aloof from group activities.

131. Fancy-dress party on La Garoupe beach, Antibes. 1926. On left Olga Picasso, holding her hand is Comte Etienne de Beaumont, and on extreme right the Comtesse de Beaumont. Picasso, not disguised, is seated in the centre.

132. Picasso with Mme Errazuriz and Olga Picasso at a ball given in Paris by the Comte Etienne de Beaumont. 1924. Photo by Man Ray.

133. Picasso: *Comte Etienne de Beaumont, the animator of les Soirées de Paris.* 1925 (lead pencil and rubber).

51

134. Picasso in his studio. 1922.
Photo by Man Ray.

136. Picasso: *Paul Valéry*. 1921.
Frontispiece for *La Jeune Parque*, Paris
(N.R.F.). (Lithograph, $7\frac{1}{8} \times 5\frac{1}{8}$.)
Col. Dr Bernhard Geiser.

137. Picasso: *Max Jacob crowned with a
laurel wreath*. 1928 (crayon).
Col. André Lefèvre.

135. Picasso: *Pierre Reverdy*. 1922.
Frontispiece for *Cravates de Chanvre*,
Paris (Editions Nord-Sud).
(Etching, $8\frac{3}{4} \times 6\frac{1}{4}$.)
Col. Dr Bernhard Geiser.

138. Picasso: *André Breton*. 1923.
Frontispiece for *Clair de Terre*, Paris
(The Author). (dry point, $11 \times 7\frac{1}{2}$.)
Col. Dr Bernhard Geiser.

139. Picasso at Juan les Pins. 1926.
Photo by Man Ray.

140. Picasso and Olga Picasso.
Cannes, 1933.

141. Picasso. *Self-portrait.* 1929 (oil, 24 × 29). Private Collection, London.

142. Picasso at 23 rue la Boétie. 1931. His left hand rests on the head of the *Jester*, a bronze of 1905. On his right is a cubist painting of 1914 and a recent sculpture in iron on which he had hung objects for his amusement. Photo by Cecil Beaton.

Cubism had never been abandoned, but in 1925 Picasso's mood became less tranquil. He began to add to his paintings an element of violence that had not appeared in earlier work. Distortions of the human form began to reveal that confidence was turning into doubt and love into estrangement, a process that found its culmination in one miserable year, 1935, when separation from his wife and recriminations drove him for the only time in his life to abandon painting. Although he did not paint, this period was marked by an outburst of poems written in both French and Spanish.

The moment of despair was fortunately brief. A year later, some months after the birth of his daughter Maia, offspring of a liaison with Marie Thérèse Walter, whose beauty had inspired the great moonlike heads in the sculpture and paintings of the early thirties, Picasso met Dora Maar. The years that followed were

143. Picasso: *Marie Thérèse Walter*.
1939 (crayon).

144. Picasso at 23 rue la Boétie. 1931.
On the wall is a recent picture by him.
Near the top appears the head in
profile of Marie Thérèse Walter.
Photo by Cecil Beaton.

fertile in inspiration. The bull fight with which he had been familiar from his early youth in Spain and its associated legends and myths, became once more vivid in his thought, forming the background of themes in which the Minotaur was both hero and victim.

Boisgeloup, La Rue des Grands Augustins and Spain

In 1932 Picasso established himself at the seventeenth-century Château de Boisgeloup in Normandy, graceful in its proportions and surrounded by noble trees. Across the courtyard there were extensive stables which he used as studios for the heads he was sculpting inspired by Marie Thérèse. Four years later he added to his overcrowded studio apartment in Paris the great rooms of the former Hotel des Ducs de Savoie in the Rue des Grands Augustins. It was there that he found sufficient space to work on the vast canvas of *Guernica*.

145. Picasso in his studio, 7 rue des
Grands Augustins. 1938.
Photo by Peter Rose Pulham.

146. Château de Boisgeloup, Gisors (Eure) bought by Picasso in 1932.

147. 7 rue des Grands Augustins, Paris. In 1937 Picasso took the two top floors of this seventeenth-century house. During the war he moved his living quarters there from the rue la Boétie.

148. Picasso: *Boisgeloup in the rain.* 1931 (oil).

149. The chapel and entrance to the château. These features appear in several landscapes.

150. Picasso at Boisgeloup. 1932. On his left Braque, Mme Braque, and his son Paulo.

151. Picasso with the painter Elie Lascaux, D-H. Kahnweiler, and Michel Leiris at Boisgeloup. 1932.

152. Picasso with his St Bernard dog at Boisgeloup. 1935.
Photo by Dora Maar.

In 1933 and again in the following year Picasso revisited Spain. The first trip took him only to Barcelona where his mother and his sister Lola, now married to Dr Vilato, were still living. The next visit took him to San Sebastian, Madrid, Toledo, and the Escurial. For the first time in twenty-five years a group of young admirers organized in 1936 an exhibition of important paintings in Barcelona which was opened by Paul Eluard. It travelled later to Bilbao and Madrid.

153. Opening of the Guernica Exhibition in aid of Spanish relief at Whitechapel by the Rt Hon. Major Attlee. 1938.

154. Picasso painting *Guernica*. 1937. Photo by Dora Maar.

Guernica

As a Spaniard and as an artist, the outbreak of the Spanish Civil War affected Picasso in the roots of his being. He at once made it clear that his sympathies lay with the Republicans by accepting the honorary directorship of the Prado. Stirred to anger by the bombing of Guernica, he composed a great painting for the Spanish Republican Pavilion in the Paris Exhibition of 1937. The picture with all the preliminary sketches was exhibited in London and in Manchester in 1938, and now hangs in the Museum of Modern Art in New York, where it has joined that earlier painting whose revolutionary significance is limited to the aesthetic plane, *Les Demoiselles d'Avignon*.

155. Picasso: *Two drawings of the left hand of the artist*. 1919 (lead pencil).

156. Picasso at work on *Guernica* mixes his colours. 1937. Photo by Dora Maar.

61

157. Picasso and Dora Maar bathing at Golfe Juan. 1937.

158. A group at the villa of Senator Cuttoli, Cap d'Antibes, 1937. From left to right, foreground, Man Ray, Picasso, Dora Maar; above, a friend, Madame Cuttoli and Senator Cuttoli. Photo by Man Ray.

159. Picasso leaving Mougins. 1937. Photo by Man Ray.

160. Picasso at Mougins. 1938.

161. Picasso with his dog Kasbec, Golfe Juan. 1937. Photo by Man Ray.

162. Picasso and Paul Eluard at Mougins. 1936.

163. Picasso at Mougins. 1935 or 1936.
Photo by Man Ray

164. Picasso: *Nusch Eluard*. 1937 (oil).
Owned by the artist.

Summer in the South of France

The summers of 1936 to 1938 were spent at Mougins. The close
friendship between Picasso and Paul Eluard coincided at this time
with Picasso's urge to write poetry and his increasing consciousness,
stirred by the Spanish war, of social and political issues. Books,
poems, and lithographs of illuminated poems were the outcome of
months spent together and Nusch the fragile and beautiful wife of
Eluard was the inspiration of many portraits, both lifelike and
fantastic.

165. Picasso, Nusch, wife of Paul
Eluard, and Dora Maar, Mougins. 1936.

63

166. Picasso: *Portrait of Dora Maar.* 1944 (lead pencil, $16\frac{1}{2} \times 12$), signed and dated later. Col. Dora Maar.

167. Picasso: *Portrait of D.M.* 1939 (gouache, $18\frac{1}{4} \times 15$). Col. André Lefèvre.

168. Picasso: *Portrait of D.M. as a bird.* 1939 ($12\frac{1}{4} \times 9\frac{1}{2}$). Galerie Berggruen, Paris.

169. Picasso in his studio at Royan. 1940. Photographed by Dora Maar. Later during the occupation the taking of pictures was forbidden.

170. Picasso's studio at Royan. 1940.

171. Picasso: *Portrait of Jaime Sabartès*. 1939 (oil, 23¾ × 18). Col. Jaime Sabartès.

172. Picasso: *Self-portrait from MS. of 'Desire Caught by the Tail', a play by Picasso*. 1943. A reading directed by Albert Camus was given in 1944. Simone de Beauvoir, Valentine Hugo, Louise and Michel Leiris, Pierre Reverdy, Jean-Paul Sartre, and other friends took part.

The Second World War

When war broke out in 1939, Picasso was staying at Antibes with Dora Maar and Sabartès. During a short visit to Paris he stored away his work in places relatively safer than his studio and then retired to Royan on the coast north of Bordeaux where he remained until October of the following year. From then on he spent the rest of the war in occupied Paris. He ignored the bribes offered by the Germans and became absorbed in the many branches of his work, painting, engraving, lithography, and sculpture. He also wrote poems and a play, *Desire Caught by the Tail*, which was given a reading in secret by a distinguished company of his literary friends in the apartment of Michel Leiris.

While the first world war had no traceable influence on the work of Picasso, the second, beginning with the Spanish Civil War, left an indelible impression. Its privations, butchery, and inhumanity dominated the atmosphere. The human form was distorted with fury. The flayed head of the bull, the cat destroying a bird, the skull, the candle, imposed themselves as appropriate subjects.

With the increasing difficulties of living in occupied Paris, Picasso abandoned the rue la Boétie and settled in to the less comfortable but more spacious rooms of the rue des Grands Augustins. During the winter months the cold made it extremely difficult to continue to work. But Picasso remained the staunch supporter of his French and Spanish friends, helping them in their clandestine projects and becoming the symbol of their hopes.

173. Picasso with his daughter Maia on Liberation Day. Paris. 26 August, 1944.

174. Picasso: *Maia*. 1944 (drawing).

175. Picasso at rue des Grands Augustins with Lee Miller, first Allied correspondent to call on him after the liberation of Paris. 1944.
Photo by Lee Miller.

176. Picasso at a window of his studio with paintings. 1944.
Photo by Lee Miller.

177. Paul and Nusch Eluard in front of *Les Pêcheurs d'Antibes*, painted by Picasso in 1939. In this painting, now in the Museum of Modern Art, New York, the towers of the Palais Grimaldi appear in the top left corner (see No.188). 1944.
Photo by Lee Miller.

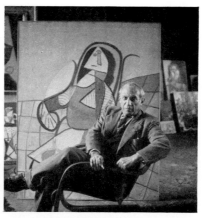

178. In Picasso's studio, left to right: Paul Eluard, Roland Penrose, Elsa Triolet, Picasso, Nusch Eluard, Louis Aragon. September 1944.
Photo by Lee Miller.

179. Picasso in his studio, rue des Grands Augustins. 1944.
Photo by Cecil Beaton.

180. Picasso and Marcel Cachin, doyen
of the French Communist Party at
'La Galloise', Vallauris. 1948. Picasso
joined the Communist Party in 1944.
He settled at the Villa La Galloise in
1948.

181. Picasso receiving a visit from
American Service personnel. 1944.
Photo by Cecil Beaton.

182. Picasso with the painter Guttuso
at the Peace Congress in Rome.
22 April 1949.

Liberation

With liberation came the return of many friends from hiding and
from abroad. For a while the studio in the rue des Grands Augustins
was invaded by those who wished to express their delight in finding
that Picasso had not only survived but that his creative vigour was
unimpaired.

At this time his sense of humanity and his desire to change the
existing injustice of society prompted him to join the French
Communist Party and to attend congresses for peace in Paris,
Rome, Warsaw, and Sheffield. In the profound hope that his

183. Picasso arriving at Sheffield with the French Deputy Gilbert Chambrun. 13 November 1950.

presence might prove to be a factor in helping to abolish future wars, he took part frequently in such demonstrations. His drawings of the dove appeared as posters on the walls of many cities, acclaimed by some as a time honoured symbol of peace and sneered at by others as an inept form of Communist propaganda, but there is no doubt about the disinterested motives of their author.

184. Picasso addressing the Sheffield Peace Congress. 1950.

185. Picasso with Dr Evatt, President of U.N.O., at the rue des Grands Augustins during the exhibition of Picasso's ceramics at the Maison de la Pensée Française. 1949.

186. Procession in the cemetery of Père Lachaise, Paris, in honour of those who died in the Resistance Movement. In the centre is Picasso. On his right Paul Eluard. 2 November, 1944.

187. Picasso among his ceramics. 1952. Photo by Robert Doisneau.

Antibes and Vallauris

When travel to the South of France again became possible, a new exhilaration made itself felt in the great luminous paintings on which he set to work in the ancient Palais Grimaldi at Antibes.

188. Le Palais Grimaldi, Antibes. In 1946 Picasso was loaned the spacious rooms of the Grimaldi Palace, centre of picture, for his studio. He worked there painting the large panels that still hang on its walls now that the building is reinstated as a museum.

189. Picasso examines a praying mantis. 1952. Photo by Robert Doisneau.

190. Claude with a drawing of him driving a toy motor by his mother Françoise Gilot. 1948. Photo by Robert Capa.

191. Picasso waits for lunch. 1952. Photo by Robert Doisneau. The rolls on the table are baked in Vallauris and known as 'Picasso's hands'.

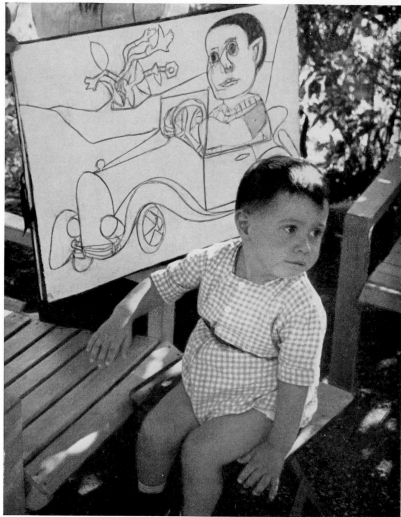

Again a sense of arcadian abandon inherited from their Mediterranean surroundings was reflected in his work.

It was at this period that his second son and second daughter, Claude and Paloma, were born. They are the children of Françoise Gilot, whose beauty and talent had drawn Picasso to her in Paris soon after liberation.

From Antibes it is only a short distance to Vallauris. In this little town, noted since the Romans for its potteries, Picasso was attracted by the skill of the local craftsmen. Trying his hand at their trade, he began at once to revolutionize their conception of ceramics and

192. Picasso: *Claude and Paloma, son and daughter of Picasso, with their mother, Françoise Gilot.* 1951 (9 × 12½). Col. Claude Gilot Picasso.

195. Picasso and Claude on the beach at Golfe Juan. 1948.
Photo by Robert Capa.

194. Picasso: *Françoise en Soleil*.
15 June 1946 (lithograph, 21 × 17¾).
Galerie Louise Leiris, Paris.

195. Françoise Gilot under an umbrella,
Picasso, and Fin Vilato, his nephew, at
Golfe Juan, 1948.
Photo by Robert Capa.

196. Interior of 'La Galloise',
Vallauris. 1953.
Photo by Alexander Liberman.

by so doing resurrected the waning fortunes of their community. He acquired at random a small and undistinguished villa *La Galloise*. From there his vast production soon invaded the nearby hangars of a disused scent factory. Sculpture and painting, including the great murals of *War and Peace*, designed for the vault of a deconsecrated chapel in the town, rapidly filled their space.

Vallauris has honoured his presence by making Picasso an honorary citizen and erecting his bronze statue of the *Homme au Mouton* in a square in the centre of the town. A local festival for the sale of local pottery and ceramics has recently become an annual event and Picasso presides at a bull fight which is attended by large numbers of his friends. These varied and continuous activities have

197. Picasso dresses up to welcome his friends. Cannes, 1956.

198. Picasso and Joan Miró at Vallauris. 1951.

199. Picasso in the arena at Nimes with left to right: Lacourière, Javier Vilato (nephew), Paul Picasso, Picasso, Castel. 1952.

200. Braque visits Picasso in his studio at Vallauris. 1954. Photo by Lee Miller.

201. Le Corbusier shows Picasso round the 'Unité d'Habitation' at Marseille. 1949.

202. Picasso visits Jacques Prévert at St Paul-de-Vence. 1953.

204. Unveiling of the statue of
L'homme au mouton at Vallauris. 1951.
The Deputy Casanova addresses the
gathering, on his right are the mayor of
Vallauris and Tristan Tzara, on his left
Picasso and Paul Eluard.

203. Picasso: *L'homme au mouton*.
1943–4 (bronze).

205. Picasso drawing with a flash-light.
Vallauris, 1949. Photo by Gjon Mili.

206. Picasso at the Madura pottery with Ramier the director. 1950. Photo by Henri Cartier Bresson.

207. Picasso with Gary Cooper and the master potter Aga at the Madura pottery at Vallauris. 1956. Photo by Lee Miller.

208. Matisse confined to his bed, but at work. On left hangs a painting given to him by Picasso. Nice. 1948. Photo by Robert Capa.

209. Wedding of Paul and Dominique
Eluard. Picasso and Françoise Gilot were
witnesses. St Tropez, 14 June 1951.
Photo by Lee Miller.

210. Picasso examines a book with,
on his right, the publisher Albert Skira,
and on his left a Spanish bullfighter,
and his son Paul. Vallauris. 1953.
Photo by Alexander Liberman.

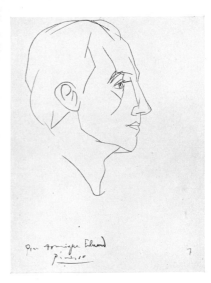

211. Picasso: *Paul Eluard* (No.7 of
fourteen portraits). 1951 (lead pencil).
Col. Mme Eluard.

not prevented visits to Paris and an unimpeded flow of a great
variety of work including sculpture, lithography, engraving, and
even the writing of poems and plays.

Although, as Sabartès remarks, the life of Picasso is usually a
matter of great regularity, his unexpected decisions to visit friends
living at a considerable distance or attend a bull fight may at any
moment break into the normal routine of his life. Such events as
the marriage of Paul Eluard at St Tropez in 1949 may be a brief
interlude or they may entice him to linger, enjoying the pleasures
of the beach and the company of his friends. In the years after the
war when Matisse was confined to his bed in Nice, Picasso paid him
frequent visits. Jacques Prévert, Jean Cocteau, and other friends
scattered along the coast welcome him often as an unexpected guest.

Visits from those who live nearby or who come from great
distances are frequent. His old friends are often given the surprise
on arrival of a display of disguises which mockingly he puts on for
their amusement. They never leave without being astonished once
more at the vigour and invention of his untiring labours. He himself brings out his canvases of all sizes and great variety. He piles
them on each other until his visitors are exhausted by their abundance. When they have left he again starts to work until late into
the night.

212. Tristan Tzara and Picasso at
Vallauris. 1951.

213. Picasso and Henri-Georges Clouzot at work filming *Le Mystère Picasso*. 1955.

214. Clouzot, Picasso, and Georges Auric, the composer of the music for the film, after the first performance. 1956.

215. Picasso with his son Paul, Christine Pauplin and Jacqueline Roque arriving for the first showing of his film. 1956.

La Californie, Cannes

After his separation from Françoise Gilot, Picasso moved to a commodious villa overlooking Cannes, surrounded by palms and eucalyptus trees. It was empty when he arrived, in the spring of 1955, but its spacious well-lit drawing rooms which have become his studio are already crowded with new paintings which synthesize the many styles and discoveries of a lifetime. In addition to this incredible production, he spent the summer of the same year working on the full length film *Le Mystère Picasso* produced by Henri-Georges Clouzot, in which he is the sole performer.

216. The studio at 'La Californie'. 1956. Photo by Lee Miller.

217. At 'La Californie', left to right, Man Ray, Julie Man Ray, the matador Minouni, Picasso, and Jacqueline Roque. 1955. Photo by Man Ray.

218. Interior of 'La Californie'. 1956. Photo by Jacqueline Roque.

219. 'La Californie' with Sabartès in the foreground. 1956.

The devotion of Jacqueline Roque, who lives beside him, makes it possible to work at the most unusual hours and at the same time receive the visits of friends. Her classical profile and her large tranquil eyes appear with many variations in the pictures piled against the walls.

To Picasso his friends and his loves are the source of his inspiration even more than the objects and the landscape around him. They continually find their way into his work in a great variety of forms. Throughout his life Sabartès reappears in varying disguises, designed for him with a malicious humour that reveals at the same time a firm affection. Among the many portraits of Dora Maar (see Nos.166, 167 and 168), which range from the grotesque architectures of Picasso's invention to faithful likenesses of her features, there are others in which he playfully sees her as a bird, just as the

221. Picasso and Jacqueline Roque at the station. Cannes, 1956. Photo by Jacqueline Roque.

222. Picasso: *Jacqueline Roque*. 30 March 1956 (crayon, 11 × 7). Galerie Rosengart, Lucerne.

face of Françoise (see No.194) appears as a flower or as the un-covered radiance of the sun, and Marie Thérèse (see No.144) takes the shape of the moon or the sleeping landscape of the earth. When he writes to his friends even on routine matters, no letter-writer has ever enlivened his paper and envelopes with decorations more calculated to enchant the receiver or more eloquent of his affection and his humanity.

In the same way that Picasso is at ease in a crowd, at a bull fight or with the local craftsmen and shopkeepers of Vallauris, he is at ease with his surroundings. He has never sought for the picturesque nor for an ideal place to live. So long as a house meets with his require-ments for work and provides a minimum of comfort, he asks for no

220. Picasso presides at the bull fight at Vallauris. On his right are Jacqueline Roque and his daughter Maia, on his left his son Claude and Jean Cocteau. 1955. Photo by Brian Brake.

223. Picasso: *Y tambien de picador* (*and also as picador*). Portrait of Sabartès. Vallauris, 26 November 1951 (pen and ink, 8¼ × 10½). Col. Jaime Sabartès.

more. To him the house is an instrument of work rather than a background for elegant living. As soon as he enters, it begins to suffer the overwhelming imprint of his presence. Every room becomes his studio or his workshop and everywhere there accumulates evidence of his activity. Objects that have found their way into his life by choice or by chance take their places indiscriminately wherever they are left and are continually joined by newcomers, while their neighbours, the objects of his own creation, increase in number incessantly. An alchemist's laboratory would be monotonous in comparison. Life is present also in the form of caged birds, dogs, and plants but the life that dominates is the great creative spirit that moves in this motley, selects, dreams, acts. Powerful energy and

224. Picasso in his studio at Vallauris. 1953. Photo by Alexander Liberman.

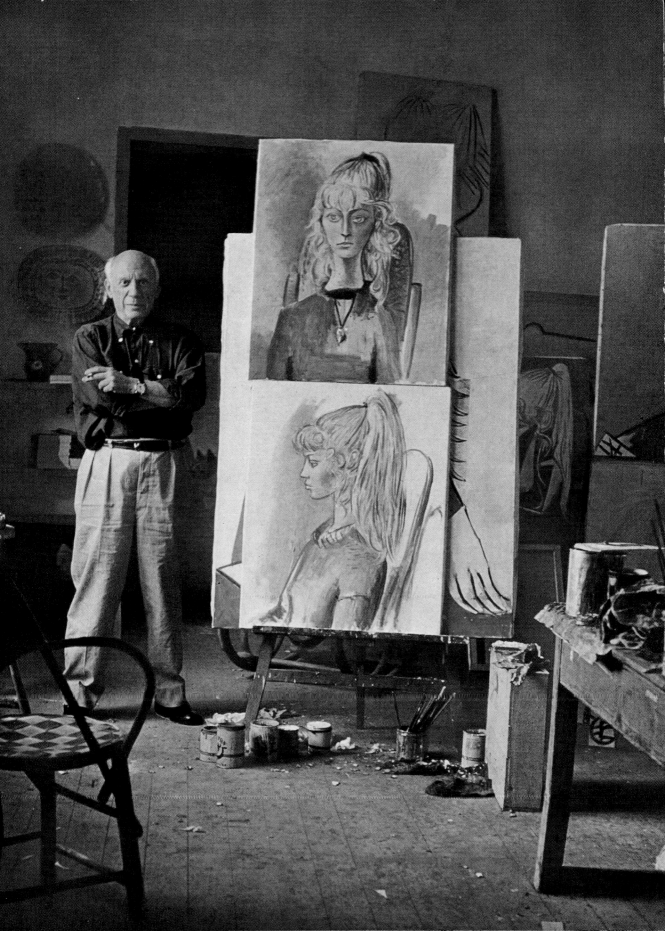

225. In the arena at Vallauris Picasso
discusses the bull fight. 1955.
Photo by Brian Brake.

precision in judgement are the Olympian qualities that rule over the
bewildering complexity of a life so prodigious in its achievements.

Since the revelation of the great painting *Les Demoiselles
d'Avignon*, the odyssey of Picasso continues. The results of his
labour are monumental and throughout the world his fame is
established as the pilot who has dared to sail chartless seas and
discover new worlds. For him the dangers that lay on all sides were
a stimulus, quickening his instincts and urging him to steer even
further from conventional routes. The storms of doubt that would

226. Photo by André Villers.

have wrecked or caused a less determined navigator to turn back
proved to be the forces that carried him towards new horizons. His
triumph lies in his generosity. The richness of his imagination and
the abundance of his energy have given to humanity a fabulous
legacy. He is the source from which inspiration continues to flow
into the world, fertilizing and enriching, heightening our degree of
consciousness and making us more acutely aware of the delights and
mysteries of our precarious existence. Our gratitude to Pablo
Picasso is immense.

227. Henri Rousseau: *Portrait de Femme.*
This early painting of Rousseau was
discovered by Picasso among piles of
rubbish in the Montmartre shop of the
Père Soulier in 1908 and bought for
five francs. Soulier, who knew it was a
Rousseau, thought it of so little value
that he told Picasso that the canvas
would be useful to him to paint over.
Picasso at once appreciated the
astonishing strength and originality of
the picture and gave it a prominent
place on the walls of his studio at the
Bateau Lavoir. It hung there above
its author during the famous banquet
given in Rousseau's honour soon after
its purchase. Picasso still claims that it
is one of the pictures he loves above
all others.

Picasso's Collection

Picasso has in his possession great quantities of paintings, sculptures,
works of art of all descriptions and objects that have appealed to him
for some vital reason. He has an intense aversion from throwing out
any object that has interested him; among his permanent treasures
are such things as banderillas given to him by a toreador, or a large
amethyst which contains a cavity half full of water mysteriously
enclosed within it. There is no sustained attempt to classify his
immense and varied collection and a great deal of it is stored away.
He has a great number of African sculptures, including some very
fine pieces and others of less monetary value, bought in the lean
years of his earliest enthusiasm for this art, which were in consequence more important in the history of the development of cubism.

Among the many paintings and sculptures that Picasso has
bought or been given are examples of the work of Le Nain, Corot,
Courbet, Gauguin, Cézanne, Renoir, the Douanier Rousseau,
Matisse, Braque, Gris, Laurens, Derain, Modigliani, Gonzales,
Manolo, Max Ernst, Man Ray, Miró, Beaudin, Balthus, Adam,
Pignon, and his father, José Ruiz Blasco.

228. Henri Rousseau (Le Douanier):
*The Representatives of Foreign Powers
come to salute the Republic in Sign of
Peace.* 1907.

229. Henri Rousseau (Le Douanier):
Portrait of the artist with a lamp.

230. Cézanne: *Le Château Noir.* 1904–6.

86

232. On the floor, a Nude (1907)
by Picasso and the head of an Ibex
by Courbet.

231. An early painting by Derain
and two early landscapes by Matisse.

234. A landscape by Gauguin, and a
painting of a pigeon by José Ruiz Blasco.

233. *Still life with oranges* by Matisse
and in the foreground the skull of
a hippopotamus.

235. A picture of a bull fight
(seventeenth-century Spanish tiles).

236. Left to right: a painting (1931)
by Picasso, a portrait by Matisse of his
daughter, Marguerite, given to
Picasso by Matisse about 1908, and a
portrait by Modigliani.

237. Corner of a mantlepiece crowded
with objects. In the centre, a bronze
by Laurens overpainted by Picasso.
On the right, *Head of a bull* in brass
by Adam.

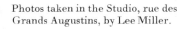

Photos taken in the Studio, rue des
Grands Augustins, by Lee Miller.

238. Balthus. Painting. 1938.

259. A glass case in the Paris studio containing rare and fragile objects. On the top shelf are tall wood sculptures of 1931, later cast in bronze, plaster casts of prehistoric female figures and the skulls of birds. On the second shelf among masks from the South Seas stands a version of the *Verre d'Absinthe*, 1914, and on the bottom shelf is a wooden hand from an Easter Island carving. Photo by Sidney Janis.

At 'La Californie' objects sometimes bought years before mingle with recent work.

240. Picasso standing at the garden entrance to his studio with a wood figure ready for casting. Cannes. Summer 1956. Photo by André Gomez.

241. Heterogeneous objects in a corner of the studio at 'La Californie', Cannes, 1956. Photo by Douglas Glass.

242. Garden sculpture at
'La Californie', cut out of sheet tin
and drawn on with chalk.
Cannes. Summer 1956.
Photo by Jacqueline Roque.

243. During the autumn of 1956
Picasso made several tall figures from
scrap pieces of packing cases, frames
and drift wood. Afterwards they were
given a permanent homogeneous form
by being cast in bronze. Cannes 1956.
Photo by Jacqueline Roque.

244. A plywood figure of a pipe-player
finds its place in the garden: Cannes,
1956. Photo by Jacqueline Roque.

245. Garden sculpture built of ceramic
tiles at 'La Californie', Cannes. Autumn
1956. Photo by Lee Miller.

246. A group of bronze heads dating
from the early 30's stand together on
the steps outside with the *Flayed Head*
of 1911 lying among them.
Cannes 1956.

Since 1954 Picasso's visits to Paris
have been rare. The great rooms
with their seventeenth-century oak
beams and tiled floors await his return.
It is in the sun of Cannes and
Vallauris that his life and work
continues.

247. The studio in the rue des Grands
Augustins, Paris, 1954.
Photo by Alexander Liberman.

248. Picasso is frequently at work in
the Madura pottery at Vallauris, near
his villa at Cannes. During the autumn
of 1956 he produced an important
series of large dishes and vases, mostly
decorated in high relief.
Vallauris. 1956.
Photo by André Gomez.

249. Work table and palette in the studio, rue des Grands Augustins, Paris, 1954.
Photo by Alexander Liberman.

250. Picasso and Alfred Barr at 'La Californie', looking at canvases that had been painted during the previous twelve months. Cannes, June 1956.
Photo by James Thrall Soby.

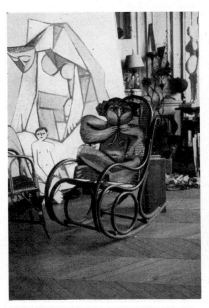

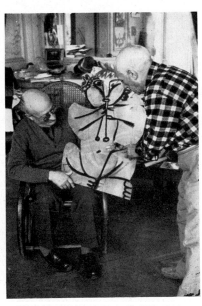

251. Picasso poses for the camera wearing a mask made of ceramic. Winter 1956.
Photo by Lee Miller.

252. Experiments in adding torn pieces of paper, objects or ornamented surfaces to pictures have led Picasso to make up figures cut out of plywood which he moves around his studio studying their relationship to furniture and the pictures against which they are seen. He enjoys the strange appearance of a faun seated in his rocking chair. Cannes, autumn 1956.
Photo by Hjalmar Boyesen.

253. Picasso and Sabartès examining a figure cut out of plywood. Winter 1956. Photo by Lee Miller.

254. Close-up view of the reproduction
of Picasso's *Massacre in Korea*
exhibited in Warsaw.

255. On a main thoroughfare in
Warsaw passers-by stop to look at a
reproduction of Picasso's picture
Massacre in Korea, displayed in
sympathy with the workers of Hungary
in November 1956.

256. Picasso with Roland Penrose at
'La Californie' in December 1956.
In the background standing on its side
can be seen the picture *Massacre in
Korea*, which had been returned
recently from a tour of exhibitions in
Paris, Munich, and Hanover.

Events in central Europe in the autumn of 1956 disturbed Picasso
deeply. Although he is not interested in politics, regarding them as
a crafty game outside his sphere, he has been a member of the
French Communist Party since 1944. When he heard, however, that
a large reproduction of the picture painted by him in 1951 to which
he gave the title *Massacre in Korea* had been exhibited in the
streets of Warsaw as a protest against the suppression of the revolt
of the Hungarian workers by Russian tanks, he welcomed the purpose to which his painting had been put by the Poles. The picture
had been painted as an outcry against war and military violence, and
its appeal was intended by him to be universal. A few days later, in
November 1956, Picasso signed a letter to the central committee of
the French Communist Party, with nine others, expressing 'profound anxiety' and denouncing the veil of silence deliberately
drawn over these events.

In the tall luminous rooms of his villa, Picasso lives surrounded by the objects he has collected with affection, the gifts that have been brought to him, and his own creations. Familiar with them, watching them constantly in the changing light, moving among them and varying their positions, he makes them play together and exchange glances like children. The strength with which he endows all that he creates in colour, line, and mass brings about a transformation. The basic material, the canvas, paint, plywood, paper, ceramic, or whatever he may use, assumes a new reality, a tenseness, a life of its own. Its presence reacts profoundly on the spectator. By means of the non-violent but eternal power of art, Picasso transmits triumphantly his message.

257. Picasso seated in front of his canvases. On the floor to the left is a decorated jar recently fired in the kilns at Vallauris, and on the right is the figure of a boy playing the pipes, cut out of plywood. Cannes 1956. Photo by Jacqueline Roque.

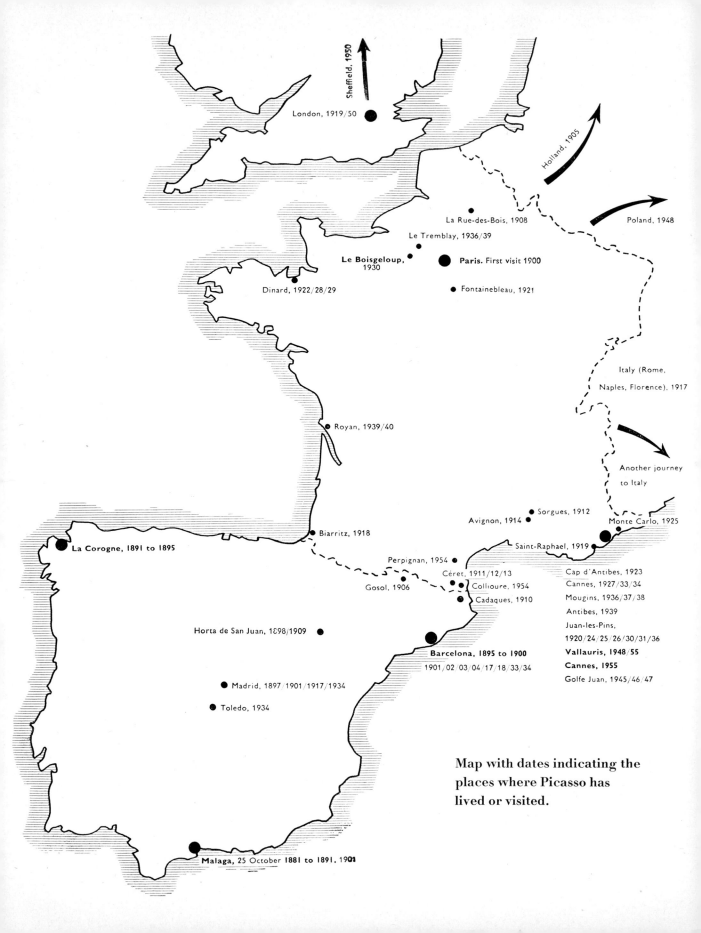

Sheffield, 1950

London, 1919/50

Holland, 1905

Poland, 1948

La Rue-des-Bois, 1908

Le Tremblay, 1936/39

Le Boisgeloup,
1930

Paris. First visit 1900

Fontainebleau, 1921

Dinard, 1922/28/29

Italy (Rome,
Naples, Florence), 1917

Royan, 1939/40

Another journey
to Italy

Sorgues, 1912

Avignon, 1914

Monte Carlo, 1925

Biarritz, 1918

Saint-Raphael, 1919

Perpignan, 1954

Céret, 1911/12/13

Cap d'Antibes, 1923

Gosol, 1906

Collioure, 1954

Cannes, 1927/33/34

Cadaques, 1910

Mougins, 1936/37/38

La Corogne, 1891 to 1895

Antibes, 1939

Juan-les-Pins,
1920/24/25/26/30/31/36

Horta de San Juan, 1898/1909

Vallauris, 1948/55

Barcelona, 1895 to 1900

Cannes, 1955

1901/02/03/04/17/18/33/34

Golfe Juan, 1945/46/47

Madrid, 1897/1901/1917/1934

Toledo, 1934

Map with dates indicating the
places where Picasso has
lived or visited.

Malaga, 25 October 1881 to 1891, 1901

Index

95

P9-CNF-751

TRANSFORMATION
OF A MAN'S HEART *SERIES*

WORK

Fil Anderson, Robert A. Fryling,
Craig M. Glass *and* Stephen W. Smith

SIX SESSIONS FOR INDIVIDUALS OR GROUPS

IVP Connect
An imprint of InterVarsity Press
Downers Grove, Illinois

InterVarsity Press
P.O. Box 1400, Downers Grove, IL 60515-1426
World Wide Web: www.ivpress.com
E-mail: mail@ivpress.com

©2006 by Stephen W. Smith

All rights reserved. No part of this book may be reproduced in any form without written permission from InterVarsity Press.

InterVarsity Press® is the book-publishing division of InterVarsity Christian Fellowship/USA®, a student movement active on campus at hundreds of universities, colleges and schools of nursing in the United States of America, and a member movement of the International Fellowship of Evangelical Students. For information about local and regional activities, write Public Relations Dept., InterVarsity Christian Fellowship/USA, 6400 Schroeder Rd., P.O. Box 7895, Madison, WI 53707-7895, or visit the IVCF website at <www.intervarsity.org>.

All Scripture quotations, unless otherwise indicated, are taken from the Holy Bible, New International Version®. NIV®. *Copyright ©1973, 1978, 1984 by International Bible Society. Used by permission of Zondervan Publishing House. All rights reserved.*

Design: Cindy Kiple
Images: Altrendo Images / Getty Images

ISBN-10: 0-8308-2149-X
ISBN-13: 978-0-8308-2149-5

Printed in the United States of America ∞

P	19	18	17	16	15	14	13	12	11	10	9	8	7	6	5	4	3	2	1
Y	21	20	19	18	17	16	15	14	13	12	11	10	09	08	07	06			

CONTENTS

INTRODUCTION

Too often we are like strangers in our own house. Asked why we think, feel and act in a certain way, we find we have no answer.

Consider, for example, our work. Our identity is caught up in what we do, but in unguarded moments we wonder whether what we do is enough to carry us through the years, to live on after us. If our strength as men is measured by our performance, what happens if our performance doesn't measure up? What happens when our strength fails us?

The journey toward transformation is all about reshaping our hearts; not the muscle in our chest but what Henri Nouwen calls "our hidden center"—often hidden even from us. We keep our distance from it, as though what holds the passion inside of us is what frightens us most.

That is the painful part of being human. We fail to know our hidden center and our submerged parts, so we live and die without knowing who we really are. We are strangers in our own house.

The four Transformation of a Man's Heart discussion guides help us to get our house in order. More than just a Bible study, these guides help us to explore the distinctives of the masculine heart and move us toward authentic transformation into the men God wants us to become.

Each session begins with an excerpt from the book *The Transformation of a Man's Heart*, compiled and edited by Stephen W. Smith.

This passage can be read individually or aloud in a group setting. It isn't necessary to read the book before going through this guide, but you may want to read the book for a more in-depth exploration of how God transforms a man's life.

Sessions are divided into five different sections, each of which helps you focus on a different aspect of your heart. "Examining My Story" offers reflective questions and exercises that help prepare us for the topic, theme and heartfelt need that will be addressed. "Engaging the Scriptures" is a guided study of a particular section of Scripture with questions and comments. "Experiencing the Journey" is a practical application of what has just been studied.

This convergence of thought, Scripture and reflection will help equip us for what lies ahead. "Expressing Our Hearts to God" offers creative ways of praying about the subject. And occasional "Encouragements from Other Companions" run alongside each session to reassure us that our experience is authentic and transformation is possible.

SUGGESTIONS FOR INDIVIDUAL USE

If you have chosen to use this guide individually, you can move at your own pace from session to session, taking as much time as you like working through the questions, journaling your responses and taking notes. Consider using a simple spiral-bound journal to elaborate on your answers. Allow yourself to reflect on the issues that are raised. Each session is designed to be a guided journey into the truth of God's Word and the issues of a man's heart.

1. As you begin each session, pray that God will speak to you through his Word.

2. Read the introduction to the session and respond to the personal reflection questions under "Examining My Story." These are designed to help you focus on God and on the theme of the session.

3. "Engaging the Scriptures" deals with a particular biblical passage. Read and reread the passage to be studied. Unless otherwise indicated, the questions are written using the language of the New International Version, so you may wish to use that version of the Bible. *The Message* is also recommended.

4. It might be good to have a Bible dictionary handy. Use it to look up any unfamiliar words, names or places.

5. Take your time working through "Experiencing the Journey." The witness of the Bible and the work of the Spirit may converge in your heart during this time. Be honest with yourself and open to change.

6. Use the prayer suggestion to guide you in thanking God for what you have learned and to pray about the applications that have come to mind.

SUGGESTIONS FOR GROUP MEMBERS

Small groups and classes make excellent forums for rich discussion; this guide will help a group get to some of the core issues facing men today. Lively discussion should be welcomed, and every member of your group should strive to create a safe environment for each other to share openly and deeply about issues of the heart.

A safe environment for men is fostered by setting certain ground rules which should be agreed on prior to the group's beginning. Here are some suggested ground rules to think through prior to beginning your group:

1. Be willing to participate in the discussion. The leader will be asking the questions that are found in this guide. The leader can really become more of a guide than a teacher, helping navigate the discussion that will result from the study. The sessions will "teach" themselves. Group members will also help teach each other.

2. Stick to the topic being discussed. This allows for everyone to par-

ticipate in in-depth study on equal ground.

3. Be sensitive to the other members of the group. Listen attentively when they describe what they have learned. You may be surprised by their insights! Many questions do not have "right" answers, particularly questions that aim at meaning or application.

4. Jesus modeled acceptance throughout his interaction with people. Paul reminds us to "accept one another just as Christ accepted you" (Romans 15:7). Feeling accepted without the threat of feeling judged is key to helping men relax and share their story and heart struggles. In the group, be affirming whenever you can. This will encourage some of the more hesitant members of the group to participate.

5. Be careful not to dominate the discussion. We are sometimes so eager to express our thoughts that we leave too little opportunity for others to respond. By all means participate! But allow others to also. Everyone needs to be heard, and if we can make sure that all hearts are heard when we do the study, we'll meet a deeper goal of actually being a "group" or community.

6. Expect God to teach you through the passage being discussed and through the other members of the group. Pray that you will have an enjoyable and profitable time together, but also that as a result of each session you will find ways that you can participate in God's work transforming your life.

7. Confidentiality is important to create a safe environment. Decide together who the group members will tell. Will spouses or other friends know what is shared in the group? Anything said in the group should not be discussed outside the group unless specific permission is given to do so.

If you are the group leader, you will find additional suggestions and help at the back of the guide.

THE PROCESS OF TRANSFORMATION

Transformation is *never* complete. I am no trophy of transformation, only a man in the process of transformation. I can only confess (and you can confess with me):

> God uses flawed men to accomplish his purposes.
> I am a flawed man.
> I am a man in process.
> God is using me now and will continue to use me in the future to accomplish what he desires.
> I am not perfect, but I am available.
> Come, O God, and transform my heart.

The real transformation of a man involves his heart. If we are to be transformed, God must have access to that sacred place within. Let the transformation begin!

WHY WORK?

Work is an inescapable reality. It's what occupies a significant portion of most of our days. It's how we manage to pay our bills. But its significance is much further reaching. It reflects our unique place in the world as God's created daughters and sons. The crucial question is whether we believe our work is part of God's original plan or a result of the rebellion of God's children.

The Bible is clear on the subject of work. "The LORD God took the man," Scripture says, "and put him in the Garden of Eden to work it and take care of it." (Gen 2:15). But after his rebellion, Adam is confronted by God: "Cursed is the ground because of you; through painful toil you will eat of it all the days of your life. . . . By the sweat of your brow you will eat your food until you return to the ground" (Gen 3:17, 19).

With this passage as a foundation, some view work as affliction, a punishment for rebellion. But for others, like me, the challenge is to bring together the necessity of work and the longing for intimacy with God.

EXAMINING MY STORY

1. What motivates you to go to work every day?

2. Does your work, at the present time, offer you a
    sense of fulfillment or leave you with a sense of
    futility? Explain.

ENGAGING THE SCRIPTURES

Genesis 1:27-31; 2:15; 3:17-19

^{1:27} So God created man in his own image,
    in the image of God he created him;
    male and female he created them.
²⁸God blessed them and said to them, "Be fruitful
and increase in number; fill the earth and subdue it.
Rule over the fish of the sea and the birds of the air and
over every living creature that moves on the ground."
    ²⁹Then God said, "I give you every seed-bearing
plant on the face of the whole earth and every tree
that has fruit with seed in it. They will be yours for
food. ³⁰And to all the beasts of the earth and all the
birds of the air and all the creatures that move on the
ground—everything that has the breath of life in
it—I give every green plant for food." And it was so.
    ³¹God saw all that he had made, and it was very
good. And there was evening, and there was morn-
ing—the sixth day.

^{2:15} The LORD God took the man and put him in the
Garden of Eden to work it and take care of it.

^{3:17} To Adam he said, "Because you listened to your

wife and ate from the tree about which I commanded you, 'You must not eat of it,'

> "Cursed is the ground because of you;
>> through painful toil you will eat of it
>> all the days of your life.
> [18]It will produce thorns and thistles for you,
>> and you will eat the plants of the field.
> [19]By the sweat of your brow
>> you will eat your food
>> until you return to the ground,
>> since from it you were taken;
>> for dust you are
>> and to dust you will return."

3. Read Genesis 1:27-31. What is Adam's job? What
    does this tell you about the nature of a man's
    work?

4. According to Genesis 3:17-19, why does a man
    work?

5. The ground and world that God made ends up
    working against the man. What is the relationship
    between work and futility that God describes here?

Some people give up early and settle for a humdrum life. Others never seem to learn, and so they flail away through a lifetime, becoming less and less human by the year, until the time they die there is hardly enough humanity left to compose a corpse.

EUGENE PETERSON

> The human approach to work can be naive, fatalistic, power-mad, money-grubbing, unenthusiastic, cynical, detached, and obsessive. It can also be selflessly mature, revelatory and life giving; mature in its long-reaching effects, and life giving in the way it gives back to an individual or society as much as it has taken. Almost always it is both, a sky full of light and dark, with all the varied weather of an individual life blowing through it.
>
> DAVID WHYTE

6. Genesis 3:17 speaks of "painful toil." How will work for man be a challenge given these circumstances and God's directive here? Describe your own experience of "painful toil."

7. Can work be fulfilling even after the curse placed on Adam? How?

8. What ought we to expect about our own experience of work, according to these passages?

EXPERIENCING THE JOURNEY

9. How is our understanding of work transformed as we grow as Christians? What difference does being a Christian make in the way we approach our job?

EXPRESSING OUR HEARTS TO GOD

David prayed in Psalm 86:11-12, "Teach me your

way, O Lord, and I will walk in your truth; give me
an undivided heart, that I may fear your name. I will
praise you, O Lord my God, with all my heart; I will
glorify your name forever."

Write or say a prayer regarding your work. Express to God your "divided" feelings about work and
life.

WHO DO I WORK FOR?

Going through the motions" is not the way of a man who's seeking God in his work and relationships. Because spirituality is a down-to-earth matter, spiritual growth is evidenced more by the smell of sweat than by the aroma of holiness and more by the calluses on our hands than the wings on our backs! When it's God I seek, there's no avoidance of hard work—manual, menial, or mental.

St. Benedict understood there's no artificial division between the sacred domain of prayer and the "worldly" activity of work. Everything in life is sacred. Prayer rightly understood is a form of work, while work is a form of prayer. It's crucial to appreciate that work is our contribution to the ongoing creation of the world and the means wherein we demonstrate that we're made in God's image.

EXAMINING MY STORY

1. What about your work feels secular? What about your work feels sacred? Explain.

2. "Work is our contribution to the ongoing creation of the world and the means wherein we demonstrate that we're made in God's

image." What does this quote mean to you?

3. How does your work contribute to the world's
    ongoing creation?

ENGAGING THE SCRIPTURES

Colossians 3:22—4:1

[3:22] Slaves, obey your earthly masters in everything;
and do it, not only when their eye is on you and to
win their favor, but with sincerity of heart and rever-
ence for the Lord. [23]Whatever you do, work at it with
all your heart, as working for the Lord, not for men,
[24]since you know that you will receive an inheritance
from the Lord as a reward. It is the Lord Christ you
are serving. [25]Anyone who does wrong will be repaid
for his wrong, and there is no favoritism.

[4:1]Masters, provide your slaves with what is right
and fair, because you know that you also have a Master in heaven.

4. What words stand out that offer you insight into
    what Paul is really saying about working rela-
    tionships?

5. One translation of this passage reads, "Work from the heart for your real Master." What does it look like to "work from the heart"?

6. "Being a Christian doesn't cover up bad work." How can a person model Christ while working for someone else?

7. What would motivate someone, Christian or not, to "do" more than the minimum in their work?

8. What does 4:1 tell you about the work of the person in charge? How are they to act? What is their standard of doing a good job?

I long to accomplish great and noble tasks, but it is my chief duty to accomplish humble tasks as though they were great and noble. The world is moved along, not only by the mighty shoves of its heroes, but also by the aggregate of the tiny pushes of each honest worker.

HELEN KELLER

EXPERIENCING THE JOURNEY

9. What difference is there, if any, between doing work for the Lord and for a boss?

10. Colossians 3:22—4:1 speaks of a high standard of ethics that should be present in our work life. Who sets the standard for our ethics at work? Our boss? Board? God? Whose standard do you find yourself following at work?

It's a shame that the only thing a man can do for eight hours a day is work. He can't eat for eight hours; he can't drink for eight hours; he can't make love for eight hours. The only thing a man can do for eight hours is work.

WILLIAM FAULKNER

11. How can your desires about fulfillment in work and the reality of your job converge? What needs to happen?

EXPRESSING OUR HEARTS TO GOD

Solomon's prayer about becoming a king (1 Kings 3:6-9) is a beautiful model prayer for asking God for help in our work. The things that Solomon asked for were given him, and we're told that God was pleased to hear Solomon's requests. Write your own prayer following Solomon's model:

God, I need help in my work. I want to ask you for . . .

I want to thank you for my job because . . .

I need specific help at work in these areas:

Please give me a heart like Solomon's that I might please you and have the right attitude in my work.

THREE

WORKING FROM THE HEART

The word *vocation* comes from the Latin word for a summons or call. The meaning of "vocation" runs deeper than a job and involves listening for a calling voice, intent on leading us to what is ours to do.

How can we know whose voice we're hearing? How can we have confidence in what it says? How can we trust our discernment about vocation?

"The voice we should listen to most as we choose a vocation," said Frederick Buechner in a graduation address, "is the voice that we might think we should listen to least, and that is the voice of our own gladness. . . . Is it making things with our hands out of wood or stone or paint or canvas? Or is it making something we hope like truth out of words? Or is it making people laugh or weep in a way that cleanses their spirit? I believe that if it is a thing that makes us truly glad, then it is a good thing and it is our thing and it is the calling voice that we were made to answer with our lives."

EXAMINING MY STORY

1. When do you feel most alive, glad and content?

2. Name the three greatest talents you believe you
    possess:

3. If you were using all three of those talents at
    once, what would you be doing?

ENGAGING THE SCRIPTURES

Exodus 31:1-11

[1]Then the LORD said to Moses, [2]"See, I have chosen
Bezalel son of Uri, the son of Hur, of the tribe of
Judah, [3]and I have filled him with the Spirit of God,
with skill, ability and knowledge in all kinds of
crafts—[4]to make artistic designs for work in gold,
silver and bronze, [5]to cut and set stones, to work in
wood, and to engage in all kinds of craftsmanship.
[6]Moreover, I have appointed Oholiab son of Ahisa-
mach, of the tribe of Dan, to help him. Also I have
given skill to all the craftsmen to make everything I
have commanded you: [7]the Tent of Meeting, the ark
of the Testimony with the atonement cover on it,
and all the other furnishings of the tent—[8]the table
and its articles, the pure gold lampstand and all its
accessories, the altar of incense, [9]the altar of burnt
offering and all its utensils, the basin with its
stand—[10]and also the woven garments, both the sa-

cred garments for Aaron the priest and the garments for his sons when they serve as priests, [11]and the anointing oil and fragrant incense for the Holy Place. They are to make them just as I commanded you."

4. What qualifications of Bezalel are mentioned in this passage?

5. How does Moses become aware of Bezalel? Is it luck? Coincidence? Being in the right place at the right time? Networking? Explain.

6. How do Bezalel's skill, experience and passion converge in his new calling and place of work?

7. What is the difference between having a skill and having a job?

Vocation does not come from a voice "out there" calling me to become something I am not. It comes from a voice "in here" calling me to be the person I was born to be, to fulfill the original selfhood given me at birth by God.

PARKER PALMER

8. Does Bezalel's job sound fulfilling to you? What do you imagine that Bezalel felt in doing his work in the temple?

Often, in order to stay alive, we have to unmake a living in order to get back to living the life we wanted for ourselves. It is the cycle of making, disintegration and remaking that is the hallmark of meaning and creative work.

DAVID WHYTE

EXPERIENCING THE JOURNEY

9. How can you discover "the voice of your own gladness?"

10. What needs of the world do you feel stirred by and motivated to help in some way?

11. What do you need to be doing to prepare yourself to enter the "place where your deep gladness meets the world's deep need?"

EXPRESSING OUR HEARTS TO GOD

Write your own prayer of confession to God using words, feelings and concepts you have explored in this session:

Dear God:

　We've learned how to make a living, but not a life:
　We've added years to life, not life to years.
　We've cleaned up the air, but polluted the soul.
　We've split an atom, but not our prejudice.
　We plan more, but accomplish less.
　We've learned to rush, but not to wait.

I thank you for . . .

I feel like . . .

I desire . . .

I'm asking you to . . .

Amen.

With hind-sight's near perfect vision, I see how often the signs of my vocation have been "hidden" in plain sight: located within the gifts and talents that are mine, the deep inner longing of my heart, and awareness of the things that make me feel most alive.

FIL ANDERSON

FOUR

THINKING THROUGH WHAT YOU RECEIVED

Get rid of your junk, or move!" For generations a family had been living in a rural area on the outskirts of the city. It had now become engulfed by relentlessly expanding suburbs. The family had a business at their home—collecting, storing and selling junk—and eventually the city issued an ultimatum. The head of that household responded, "It's unfair! Our family has been collecting junk for years. It's all we know."

A lot of our families are like that. We've been collecting junk for years; it's all we know. We collect wounded relational habits, dysfunctional communication patterns or sinful lifestyles. They become an accepted way of living which may, in fact, seem normal to us. A man leaves a legacy for those who live beyond him—not just his children, but his friends, neighbors, coworkers and family. A godly man leaves a good legacy. An unintentional man passes on junk.

EXAMINING MY STORY

1. What has been "passed on" to you by your parents, grandparents or guardians? Write down some key words or specific values.

2. How would you categorize the list you made?
   Junk? Valuable? Irreplaceable? Explain.

ENGAGING THE SCRIPTURES

2 Timothy 1:1-7

[1]Paul, an apostle of Christ Jesus by the will of God, according to the promise of life that is in Christ Jesus,

[2]To Timothy, my dear son:

Grace, mercy and peace from God the Father and Christ Jesus our Lord.

[3]I thank God, whom I serve, as my forefathers did, with a clear conscience, as night and day I constantly remember you in my prayers. [4]Recalling your tears, I long to see you, so that I may be filled with joy. [5]I have been reminded of your sincere faith, which first lived in your grandmother Lois and in your mother Eunice and, I am persuaded, now lives in you also. [6]For this reason I remind you to fan into flame the gift of God, which is in you through the laying on of my hands. [7]For God did not give us a spirit of timidity, but a spirit of power, of love and of self-discipline.

3. How does Paul refer to Timothy? What does this imply about their relationship?

4. In verse 3, Paul refers to "forefathers." What can we know about Paul's spiritual legacy?

5. Who are the specific people that Paul points out to Timothy? What did Timothy get from them?

6. Why do you think Paul found it important to remind Timothy of his "faith-legacy" and responsibility?

Monuments, legacies, marks— that's where we always go wrong. We're here to revel in the world, to soak in the awesomeness of it, to enjoy the ride.

DEAN KOONTZ

7. What does a person do to "fan into flame" the gift God has given us?

8. Read verse 7 again. What does the context of this passage reveal about Paul's words here?

EXPERIENCING THE JOURNEY

9. What spiritual role models encourage you in your Christian walk today? How do these specific people help you?

10. Not all of us have the "faith-legacy" that Timothy enjoyed in his family. What people outside of your family has God used to help shape your faith?

11. How can the members of the group help to "fan the flame" of your gift and faith? What specific things do you need from the group members that can help you in your journey?

EXPRESSING OUR HEARTS TO GOD

In Psalm 139:13-15, David gives thanks for how God made him. Read these verses (from *The Message*) out loud as a prayer of thanksgiving to God.

Oh yes, you shaped me first inside, then out;
    you formed me in my mother's womb.
I thank you, High God—you're breathtaking!
Body and soul, I am marvelously made!
I worship in adoration—what a creation!
You know me inside and out,
    you know every bone in my body;
You know exactly how I was made, bit by bit,
how I was sculpted from nothing into
    something.

WEAK IN OUR FAILURES, STRONG IN OUR HEARTS

Failure for most of us is a messy and traumatic realization that something has gone wrong in our life. For some it is a failed marriage or failed parenting, but for many men our most debilitating times of failure are connected with job loss because our masculine identity is so strongly associated with our work. We are proud of what we do and what we accomplish. When we lose our role for whatever reason we become disoriented in who we are. We often feel defensive or inadequate or both. Rarely do we anticipate that failure can be a gateway to spiritual transformation.

Spiritual transformation is not a one-time event. As the apostle Paul predicted, it is an ongoing process of being conformed to the image of Christ (2 Corinthians 3:18). Being fired from a job does not transform us per se, but it forces us to look internally and see what is happening in our soul. A traumatic testing is also a touch of grace that gives us time to be more intentionally aware of God's transforming work in our life—and especially in our heart.

EXAMINING MY STORY

1. Why do you believe books on success outnumber books on failure? Why is failure harder to address?

2. How do people who fail at something get treated by their friends? the church? the culture?

3. How has God used a failure to bring about transformation in your heart?

> *Life isn't easy. Neither is spiritual transformation. Like clay whirling on the potter's wheel, it's a messy process.*
>
> **STEPHEN W. SMITH**

ENGAGING THE SCRIPTURES

2 Corinthians 12:7-10

[7]To keep me from becoming conceited because of these surpassingly great revelations, there was given me a thorn in my flesh, a messenger of Satan, to torment me. [8]Three times I pleaded with the Lord to take it away from me. [9]But he said to me, "My grace is sufficient for you, for my power is made perfect in weakness." Therefore I will boast all the more gladly about my weaknesses, so that Christ's power may rest on me. [10]That is why, for Christ's sake, I delight in weaknesses, in insults, in hardships, in persecutions, in difficulties. For when I am weak, then I am strong.

4. Does Paul speak more of success in these verses or failure? Why? What is he trying to tell us?

5. What was Paul asking of God?

6. Describe the process that Paul endured. How did Paul handle the experience of unanswered prayer?

Here in this "place," God is at work, bending, breaking, molding, doing just as he chooses. Why he is doing it, we do not know; he is doing it for one purpose only—that he is able to say, "This is my man. . ."

OSWALD CHAMBERS

7. Weakness and strength are mentioned in the same place in verse 10. How can weakness and strength coexist?

8. What does it look like to boast in weaknesses?

EXPERIENCING THE JOURNEY

9. Think of some other biblical characters who experienced some kind of failure. How did God transform their failure?

10. Describe the "residue" that failure leaves on a man's heart.

A [person] who fails well is greater than one who succeeds badly.

THOMAS MERTON

11. What do you do when you feel condemned by your own conscience or nagging guilt about a failure?

EXPRESSING OUR HEARTS TO GOD

Ruth Myers offers the following prayer as a way of seeing our challenges through the eyes of faith:

"Thank you that you have me in the place You want me just now . . . that even if I got there through wrong choices or indifference or even re-

bellion, yet You knew my mistakes and sins before I ever existed, and You worked them into your plan to draw me to Yourself, to mold and bless me and to bless others through me. Thank you that, even if I'm here through the ill-will or poor judgment of other people, all is well; for in Your sovereign wisdom, You are at work to bring about good results from all those past decisions, those past events beyond my control—good results both for me and for others."

Put this prayer into your own words.

LEAVING YOUR LEGACY NOW, NOT LATER

A few years ago my father called and said, "I'm going down to my old neighborhood today and visiting my parents' gravesite. Do you want to come along?" I jumped at the opportunity. Finding the street where he grew up, Dad pointed out his house and where he and his pals played softball and football in the street. We found our way to the cemetery where his dad and mom are buried, and stood in silence by the two gravesites, pondering those two lives that had made such a profound impact on my father's own. Finally, Dad prayed a relatively short prayer, ending with five words that have stood out to me ever since: "Lord, I have no regrets."

A man, almost eighty years old, who can say that he has no regrets. Remarkable. I realized I had embarked on a trip into the past with my father; that he has a long and deep story; a story that is the preface of my own.

EXAMINING MY STORY

1. When you think of growing old, what emotions surface in your heart?

2. If you could write your own epitaph, what would it say?

One of the primary goals in our lives should be to prepare for our last day. The legacy we leave is not just in our possessions, but in the quality of our lives. What preparations should we be making now? The greatest waste in all of our earth, which cannot be recycled or reclaimed, is our waste of the time that God has given us each day.

BILLY GRAHAM

ENGAGING THE SCRIPTURES

Psalm 71:6-21

[6]From birth I have relied on you;
    you brought me forth from my mother's womb.
    I will ever praise you.
[7]I have become like a portent to many,
    but you are my strong refuge.
[8]My mouth is filled with your praise,
    declaring your splendor all day long.

[9]Do not cast me away when I am old;
    do not forsake me when my strength is gone.
[10]For my enemies speak against me;
    those who wait to kill me conspire together.
[11]They say, "God has forsaken him;
    pursue him and seize him,
    for no one will rescue him."
[12]Be not far from me, O God;
    come quickly, O my God, to help me.
[13]May my accusers perish in shame;
    may those who want to harm me
    be covered with scorn and disgrace.

[14]But as for me, I will always have hope;
    I will praise you more and more.
[15]My mouth will tell of your righteousness,

of your salvation all day long,
    though I know not its measure.
[16]I will come and proclaim your mighty acts,
        O Sovereign LORD;
    I will proclaim your righteousness, yours alone.
[17]Since my youth, O God, you have taught me,
    and to this day I declare your marvelous deeds.
[18]Even when I am old and gray,
    do not forsake me, O God,
    till I declare your power to the next generation,
    your might to all who are to come.

[19]Your righteousness reaches to the skies, O God,
    you who have done great things.
    Who, O God, is like you?
[20]Though you have made me see troubles, many
        and bitter,
    you will restore my life again;
    from the depths of the earth
    you will again bring me up.
[21]You will increase my honor
    and comfort me once again.

The strength of a man's virtue must not be measured by his occasional efforts, but by his ordinary life.

BLAISE PASCAL

3. How does the psalmist describe his youth?

4. What does he specifically ask God for?

5. List the descriptive words the psalmist uses to confess his faith in God. What role does God have in his life?

6. Verse 18 is a plea and prayer for a legacy of faith. Put his prayer into your own words.

7. What is the dominant theme of this psalm? What does the psalmist want?

All men die,

few men really live.

WILLIAM WALLACE
IN *BRAVEHEART*

EXPERIENCING THE JOURNEY

8. List three of God's "mighty acts," "marvelous deeds" and "righteous acts" in your life so far.

9. Who could you invite on a tour of your own faith-legacy? What would you hope for them to gain from the experience?

EXPRESSING OUR HEARTS TO GOD

Leaving a godly legacy requires having a wise heart.
Write a prayer expressing your desire to be a wise
and transformed man.

LEADER'S NOTES

Leading a group discussion can be an enjoyable and rewarding experience. But it can also be *scary*—especially if you've never done it before.

You don't need to be an expert on the Bible or a trained teacher to lead a Bible discussion. These studies are designed to be led easily. As a matter of fact, the flow of questions is so natural that you may feel that the studies lead themselves. Nevertheless, there are some important facts to know about group dynamics and encouraging discussion. The suggestions listed below should enable you to effectively and enjoyably fulfill your role as leader.

COMPONENTS OF SMALL GROUPS

A healthy small group should do more than study the Bible. There are four components to consider as you structure your time together.

Nurture. Small groups help us to grow in our knowledge and love of God. Bible study is important for making this happen.

Community. Small groups are a great place to develop deep friendships with other Christians. Allow time for informal interaction before and after each study. Plan activities and games that will help you get to know each other. Spend time having fun together.

Worship and prayer. Your study will be enhanced by spending time praising God together in prayer or song. Pray for each other's

needs—and keep track of how God is answering prayer in your group. Ask God to help you to apply what you are learning together.

Outreach. Reaching out to others can be a practical way of applying what you are learning, and it will keep your group from becoming self-focused. Consider together what other men in your lives would benefit from your group experience, and encourage participants to invite and welcome newcomers at appropriate moments in the life of your group.

PREPARING FOR THE STUDY

1. Pray for the various members of the group—including yourself. Ask God to open your hearts to the message of his Word and motivate you to action.

2. As you prepare for each session, read and reread the assigned Bible passage to familiarize yourself with it. Look at the passage in multiple translations; you can do so quickly by using Bible Gateway online <www.biblegateway.com>.

3. Carefully work through each question in the session. Spend some time alone sitting quietly before God, asking him to lead you into creative ways of guiding the group and even your own heart.

4. Write your thoughts and responses in the space provided in the guide. This will help you to express yourself clearly.

5. It might help to have a Bible dictionary handy. Use it to look up any unfamiliar words, names or places.

6. Remember that the group will follow your lead in responding to these sessions. They will not go any deeper than you do.

7. Once you have finished your own study of the passage, familiarize yourself with the leader's notes for the study you are leading.

These are designed to help you in several ways. First, they tell you the purpose the author had in mind when writing the study. Take time to think through how the study questions work together to accomplish that purpose. Second, the notes provide you with additional background information or suggestions on group dynamics for various questions. This information can be useful when people have difficulty understanding or answering a question. Third, the leader's notes can alert you to potential problems you may encounter during the study.

8. If you wish to remind yourself of anything mentioned in the leader's notes, make a note to yourself below that question in the study.

LEADING THE STUDY

1. Begin the study on time. Open with prayer.

2. Be sure that everyone in your group has a study guide.

3. At the beginning of your first time together, explain that these sessions are meant to be discussions, not lectures. Encourage the members of the group to participate. However, do not put pressure on those who may be hesitant to speak during the first few sessions. You may want to suggest the following guidelines to your group:

   • Stick to the topic being discussed.

   • Anything said in the group is considered confidential and will not be discussed outside the group unless specific permission is given to do so.

   • Listen attentively to each other and provide time for each person present to talk.

   • Pray for each other.

4. Have a group member read the introduction at the beginning of the discussion.

5. Every session begins with questions to introduce the theme of the session and encourage group members to begin to open up. Either allow a time of silence for people to respond individually or discuss it together. Be ready to get the discussion going with your own response. You may want to supplement the group discussion question with an icebreaker to help people to get comfortable.

6. Have a group member (or members, if the passage is long) read aloud the passage to be studied. Then give people several minutes to read the passage again silently so that they can take it all in.

7. As you ask the questions, keep in mind that they are designed to be used just as they are written. You may simply read them aloud. Or you may prefer to express them in your own words. There may be times when it is appropriate to deviate from the study guide. For example, a question may have already been answered. If so, move on to the next question. Or someone may raise an important question not covered in the guide. Take time to discuss it, but try to keep the group from going off on tangents.

8. Avoid answering your own questions. If necessary, repeat or rephrase them until they are clearly understood. Or point out something you read in the leader's notes to clarify the context or meaning. An eager group quickly becomes passive and silent if they think the leader will do most of the talking.

9. Don't be afraid of silence. People may need time to think about the question before formulating their answers.

10. Don't be content with just one answer. Ask, "What do the rest of

you think?" or "Anything else?" until several people have given answers to the question.

11. Acknowledge all contributions. Try to be affirming whenever possible. Never reject an answer. If it is clearly off-base, ask, "What do the rest of you think?"

12. Don't expect every answer to be addressed to you, even though this will probably happen at first. As group members become more at ease, they will begin to truly interact with each other. This is one sign of healthy discussion.

13. Don't be afraid of controversy. It can be very stimulating. If you don't resolve an issue completely, don't be frustrated. Move on and keep it in mind for later. A subsequent study may solve the problem.

14. Periodically summarize what the group has said. This helps to draw together the various ideas mentioned and gives continuity to the group. But don't preach.

15. You may want to allow group members a time of quiet for "Experiencing the Journey" or "Expressing Our Hearts to God." Then discuss what you experienced. A simple way to do this is to ask the group to pray for a few moments in silence. Then, after an appropriate amount of time, just ask, "What did you tell God?" Or you may want to encourage group members to work on these ideas between meetings. Give an opportunity during the session for people to talk about what they are learning.

16. Conclude your time together with conversational prayer, adapting the prayer suggestion at the end of the study to your group. Ask for God's help in following through on the commitments you've made.

17. End on time.

THE VERY FIRST MEETING IS IMPORTANT!

Often, it's what happens in the initial meeting that determines the culture of the group. Here's a simple outline of the first group meeting.

1. Plan on addressing some or all of the ground rules. Decide how the group will function.

2. Make sure each group member has his own guide to use.

3. Read through the introduction to the guide as a group.

4. Ask an introductory question to help foster sharing:

   • What are your expectations about being in a group like this, studying a topic like this?

   • When you look at this topic, what gets stirred up inside of you?

   • What does your wife or girlfriend, if you have one, think about your studying this?

You're ready to begin the journey toward transformation!

SESSION ONE: *Why Work?*

Question 3. Work is God's idea. We became coworkers with God in his creation, and thus we become "like" him by working. God worked in creation and we continue the work now.

Question 4. Work becomes toilsome after the Fall. In God's original design we were always to be caretakers of God's creation and work. However, the devastating effects of the Fall is seen in the toil and futility we experience as a result of sin.

Question 6. Eugene Peterson offers a paraphrase of this verse in *The*

Message: "You'll be working in pain all your life long." In this passage, we see the pain and agony of childbirth from a woman's perspective being compared to the pain and agony of how a man experiences work. Childbirth is not "just" a beautiful experience. There is pain, agony, suffering and moans in childbirth. So there is in work.

SESSION TWO: *Who Do I Work For?*

Question 4. Read the passage from several different translations. Paul doesn't condone or endorse slavery. Paul speaks directly into the real life situation of his readers. While this important passage of Scripture is written to slaves and servants, it certainly has important insight into the posture of a man's heart in doing work.

Question 5. This kind of attitude surely requires a deep transformation of the heart. Have group members list creative ways people around them engage their work with passion and energy. See also Colossians 3:17 for more insight and consideration.

Question 7. You may want to discuss real expectations versus impositions placed on the Christian in the workplace. At what point might Christian convictions come into conflict with the standard set in the workplace?

Question 11. Offer group members time to sit with this question. Invite them to journal or make a chart describing their own journey of convergence in terms of work. Reflecting back on a person's gifts and talents, previous experience, passions and desires may be helpful to process this more.

"Expressing Our Hearts to God." It would be helpful to read this from several translations. *The Message* offers us earthy language to

consider in asking God for help in our work: "I don't know the ropes, hardly know the 'ins' and 'outs' of this job. And here I am . . ."

SESSION THREE: *Working from the Heart*

Introduction. Quoted from Ken Gire, *Windows of the Soul: Experiencing God in New Ways* (Grand Rapids, Mich.: Zondervan, 1996), p. 71.

Question 4. Explore how being skilled and being spiritual intersect on the journey toward being a transformed man.

Question 5. Excellence is rewarded in this passage. Bezalel was noticed by God for all the qualities that are mentioned. God gave him the very important task of doing finely skilled work that would be required for Israel's worship.

Question 6. "Convergence" suggests different things coming together. Skill, experience, gifting, opportunity, passion and desire are all different aspects of our work. When there is convergence in many of these, drudgery can be transformed into something "more."

Question 8. If the group is unaware of what the tabernacle looked like, read Exodus 26; 27:21; and 29:42-43. This was no ordinary place. This would be the place where God would dwell.

Question 9. Consider reading *Let Your Life Speak* by Parker Palmer (Seattle: Jossey-Bass, 1999) for a more thorough self-study on vocation and gladness. David Whyte's book *Crossing the Unknown Sea* (New York: Penguin Putnam, 2001) is also helpful to explore how our journey into work is similar to a pilgrimage.

"Expressing Our Hearts to God." As quoted by Fil Anderson *in Run-*

ning on Empty: Contemplative Spirituality for Overachievers (Colorado Springs: Waterbrook, 2004), p. 17.

SESSION FOUR: *Thinking Through What You Received*

Question 2. Some participants may struggle with this question. Often, we don't want to have to think through painful parts of our past, especially when they feel raw and unresolved. Have your group make three columns on a sheet of paper. One column heading would be "Junk I Received," the second heading would be "What I Received I Like" and the third column would be "Still Deciding about This Area."

Question 4. See Philippians 3:3-11 for Paul's own words about his faith-legacy. Yet, with all that Paul received in his Jewish faith, something very important was missing. It was not until he met Jesus Christ that his whole "faith-legacy" took a new direction.

Question 9. For more understanding of how our past influences us and ways to explore this, see Stephen W. Smith, *Soul Shaping: A Practical Guide for Spiritual Transformation*, available at <www.potters inn.com>.

Question 10. Teachers, coaches, Sunday School teachers, pastors, missionaries, friends and authors can all be used by God to encourage us in the process of transformation. Be prepared to offer two or three people who significantly shaped your understanding of being a Christan.

Question 11. See in 2 Timothy 1:16-18 for Paul's example of someone who helped and encouraged him in Onesiphorus. Have the group list the things that Onesiphorus did for Paul. Challenge the group to read 2 Timothy independently in light of legacy, noting the specific instructions Paul gives to Timothy.

SESSION FIVE: *Weak in Our Failures, Strong in Our Hearts*

Question 3. Encourage group members to be specific—getting fired, going through a divorce, breaking a promise. Give a personal example of how God brought transformation in you.

Question 5. No one is really sure about what Paul is referring to in this passage. Some have suggested poor health, poor eyesight or even a person. Regardless of what the exact situation was, it resulted in a crisis for Paul.

Question 7. Explore what the paradox of weakness turning into strength looks like in contemporary life.

Question 9. It's hard to read the Scriptures without seeing God redeeming failed actions, failed relationships, failed promises, failed attempts and failed faith. It's the story of redemption. We have our own stories to add to the long list of men and women who failed but whom God redeemed.

Question 10. Possible responses include an erosion of confidence, a sense of defeat or guilt, and a loss of joy. Some experiences leave us feeling tainted rather than clean. We can feel unclean and spoiled rather than forgiven, clean and available for God to use us.

Question 11. Feeling condemned when you experience repeated failure isn't new. Paul describes this for us in Romans 8. Martin Luther advises Christians to consider our failures an opportunity to revel in "God's fatherly goodness toward me, that He so loved the world that He gave His only-begotten Son that whosoever believeth in Him should not perish, but have everlasting life. In calling me a sinner, Satan, you really comfort me above measure" (*Martin Luther's Commentary on Galatians*, <www.studylight.org/com/mlg/view.cgi?book=ga&chapter=001>).

"Expressing Our Hearts to God." Quoted from Ruth Myers, *31 Days of Praise* (Sisters, Ore.: Multnomah, 1994), p. 78.

SESSION SIX: *Leaving Your Legacy Now, Not Later*

Question 2. Have group members sit with this question for a few moments. Don't be afraid of the silence. They'll need time to write a few words that might summarize their life! Give each person a minute to share their "epitaph."

Question 3. See verses 6, 17. The psalmist discusses his inheritance, the things he has received, as he shares his story.

Question 7. This is a psalm of hope. See verse 14. The psalmist is praying these words in old age and when enemies are confronting him.

TRANSFORMATION OF A MAN'S HEART *SERIES*

The Transformation of a Man's Heart series puts men in conversation with God and with one another to see how God shapes us in the ordinary experiences of our lives. The book, featuring reflections on the masculine journey by experts in a variety of fields, can be read independently or in concert with the four discussion guides, which look in depth at the role of sex, marriage, work and transformation in the spiritual lives of men.

Each guide has six sessions, suitable for personal reflection or group discussion and based on essays in the book *The Transformation of a Man's Heart.*

SEX

For all the attention we give it, sex remains a mystery. This discussion guide by Stephen W. Smith and John D. Pierce looks at sex as part of a man's transformational journey and explores how our sexual story can inform our understanding of God and his love for us.

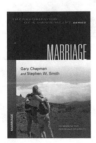

MARRIAGE

This discussion guide by Stephen W. Smith and Gary D. Chapman demystifies marriage for men, helping us see through the euphoria that led us to marry and the disillusionment that plagues us when our marriages don't turn out as we planned.

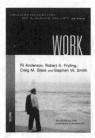

WORK

This discussion guide by Stephen W. Smith, Fil Anderson, Robert A. Fryling and Craig Glass puts men's vocational lives—their calling, their failings, their inheritance and their legacy—into the context of their relationship with God.

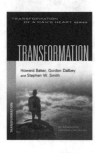

TRANSFORMATION

In this discussion guide by Stephen W. Smith, Gordon Dalbey and Howard Baker, men will be reminded that wherever they find themselves, God is there with them, inviting them out of their woundedness and onto a new and better path.

Life is many things, but it is definitely not a flow chart. We prove it every day. We deeply long for change, but formulas and seminars don't get it done. The good news is, God is at work across the life span, encouraging us and empowering us to overcome the hurdles of our past, the challenges of our present and the fears of our future.

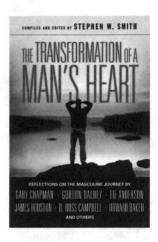

The Transformation of a Man's Heart is a book of stories: twelve men write from their hearts about their own journey toward transformation.

- Gary Chapman, author of **The Five Love Languages,** shares his journey toward experiencing a transformed marriage with his wife.

- Ross Campbell, Christian psychiatrist and author of **How to Really Love Your Child**, discusses his heart's transformation in growing as a father with his children.

- Gordon Dalbey pioneered the men's movement in his **Healing the Masculine Soul.** Here he shares how our past must be transformed in order to experience all God has for us as men.

- James Houston, mentor and friend to many Christian leaders throughout the world. considers how his own journey toward transformation reflects the call God places on every man's heart.

These and other leading men in their fields come alongside you in *The Transformation of a Man's Heart,* telling you their stories and pointing you toward the God who in the beginning wrote each of us a happy ending.

"This book is full of stories. Some will make you think.
Others will make you cry. Still others will make you kneel.
All will make you want to be a better man."
FROM THE FOREWORD BY KEN GIRE, AUTHOR OF THE DIVINE EMBRACE

Potter's Inn is a Christian ministry founded by Stephen W. and Gwen Harding Smith, and is dedicated to the work of spiritual formation. A resource to the local church, organizations and individuals, Potter's Inn promotes the themes of spiritual transformation to Christians on the journey of spiritual formation by offering

- guided retreats
- soul care
- books, small group guides, works of art and other resources that explore spiritual transformation

Steve and Gwen travel throughout the United States and the world offering spiritual direction, soul care and ministry to people who long for a deeper intimacy with God. Steve is the author of *Embracing Soul Care: Making Space for What Matters Most* (Kregel, 2006) and *Soul Shaping: A Practical Guide to Spiritual Transformation.*

Potter's Inn at ASPEN RIDGE is a 35-acre ranch and retreat nestled in the Colorado Rockies near Colorado Springs, CO. As a small, intimate retreat, Potter's Inn at Aspen Ridge is available for individual and small group retreats. "Soul Care Intensives"—guided retreats with spiritual direction—are available for leaders in the ministry and the marketplace.

For more information or to for a closer look at our artwork and literature, visit our website: www.pottersinn.com

Or contact us at

Potter's Inn
6660 Delmonico Drive, Suite D-180
Colorado Springs, CO 80919
Telephone: 719-264-8837
Email: resources@pottersinn.com